Let's get started!

How to use this book

These pages make sure we're ready for the unit ahead. Find out what we'll be learning and brush up on your skills!

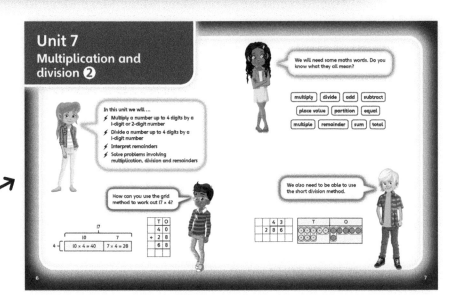

Discover

Lessons start with **Discover**.

Here, we explore new maths problems.

Can you work out how to find the answer?

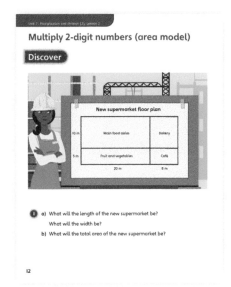

Don't be afraid to make mistakes. Learn from them and try again!

Share

Next, we share our ideas with the class.

Did we all solve the problems the same way? What ideas can you try?

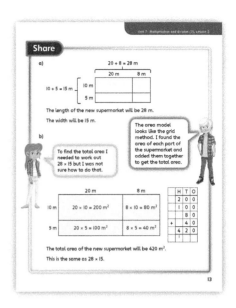

Think together

Then we have a go at some more problems together. Use what you have just learnt to help you.

We'll try a challenge too!

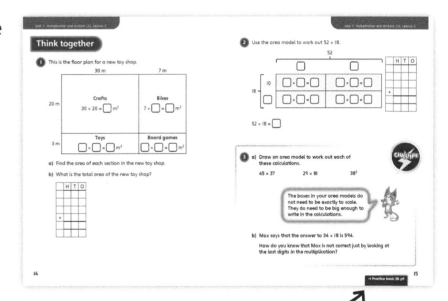

This tells you which page to go to in your **Practice Book**.

At the end of each unit there's an **End of unit check**. This is our chance to show how much we have learnt.

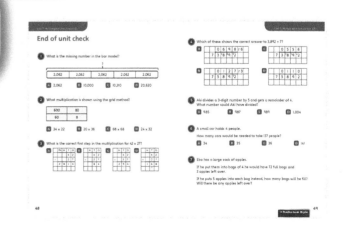

Unit 7
Multiplication and division ②

In this unit we will ...

⚡ Multiply a number up to 4 digits by a I-digit or 2-digit number

⚡ Divide a number up to 4 digits by a I-digit number

⚡ Interpret remainders

⚡ Solve problems involving multiplication, division and remainders

How can you use the grid method to work out 17 × 4?

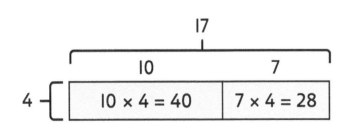

17

10	7
10 × 4 = 40	7 × 4 = 28

4

	T	O
	4	0
+	2	8
	6	8

Power Maths

Year 5
Textbook 5B

White Rose Maths

White Rose Maths Edition

Dexter

Dexter is determined.

When he makes a mistake, he learns from it and tries again.

flexible

helpful

curious

brave

Flo

Sparks

Ash

Astrid

Series editor: Tony Staneff Lead author: Josh Lury

Consultants (first edition): Professor Liu Jian and Professor Zhang Dan

Author team (first edition): Tony Staneff, Josh Lury, Timothy Weal, Neil Jarrett, Caroline Hamilton, Faye Hirst, Stephanie Kirk, Emily Fox, Zhu Dejiang and Zhu Yuhong

Pearson

Contents

Your teacher will tell you which page you need.

2

We will need some maths words. Do you know what they all mean?

| multiply | divide | add | subtract |

| place value | partition | equal |

| multiple | remainder | sum | total |

We also need to be able to use the short division method.

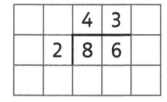

		4	3
	2	8	6

T	O

Multiply a number up to 4-digits by a 1-digit number

Discover

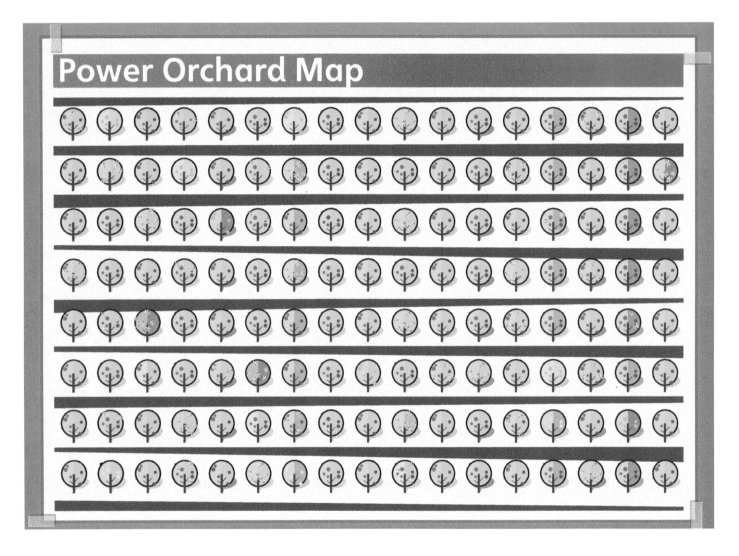

1 a) Use an array method to calculate how many trees there are in total.

b) Use a written method to calculate the number of trees.

Share

a) There are 8 rows of trees, with 17 trees in each row.

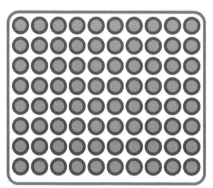 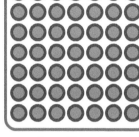

$8 \times 10 = 80$ $8 \times 7 = 56$

$80 + 56 = 136$

I used counters to represent the trees. I partitioned the counters into sections to make it easier for me to work out the total.

b)

	H	T	O
		1	7
×			8
			6
		5	

	H	T	O
		1	7
×			8
	1	3	6
		5	

I used the column method that we did last year. This is called formal column multiplication.

There are 136 trees in total.

Think together

1 Use the mathematical equipment to help you work out these multiplications.

a) 26 × 4

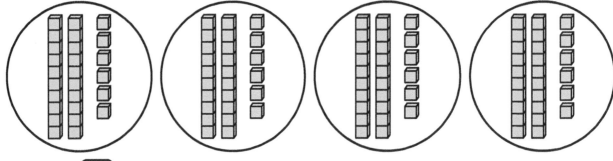

20 × 4 = ☐

6 × 4 = ☐

☐ + ☐ = ☐

b) 135 × 5 = ☐

H	T	O
100	10 10 10	1 1 1 1 1 1
100	10 10 10	1 1 1 1 1 1
100	10 10 10	1 1 1 1 1 1
100	10 10 10	1 1 1 1 1 1
100	10 10 10	1 1 1 1 1 1

100 × 5 = ☐

30 × 5 = ☐

5 × 5 = ☐

2 Complete the multiplications.

a) $42 \times 7 = \boxed{}$

	T	O
	4	2
×		7

b) $142 \times 7 = \boxed{}$

	H	T	O
	1	4	2
×			7

c) $3,142 \times 7 = \boxed{}$

	Th	H	T	O
	3	1	4	2
×				7

3 Danny and Zac are representing calculations using bar models.

CHALLENGE

What calculations are being represented? Work out the answers.

a)

Danny

?

3,285	3,285	3,285

b)

Zac

329	329	329	329	329	329

?

658	658	658	658	658

To work out Zac's calculation, I think I need to do two multiplications.

I think I can do it as just one multiplication.

11

Multiply 2-digit numbers (area model)

Discover

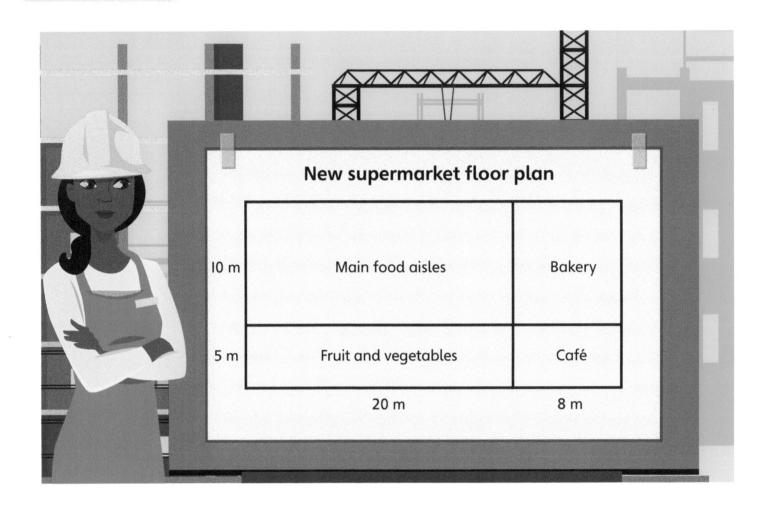

1 a) What will the length of the new supermarket be?

What will the width be?

b) What will the total area of the new supermarket be?

Share

a)

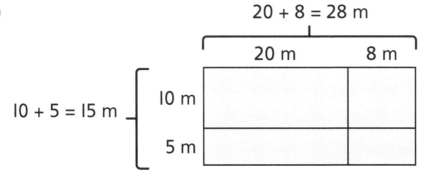

$20 + 8 = 28$ m

20 m   8 m

$10 + 5 = 15$ m

10 m

5 m

The length of the new supermarket will be 28 m.

The width will be 15 m.

The area model looks like the grid method. I found the area of each part of the supermarket and added them together to get the total area.

b)

To find the total area I needed to work out 28×15 but I was not sure how to do that.

	20 m	8 m
10 m	$20 \times 10 = 200$ m^2	$8 \times 10 = 80$ m^2
5 m	$20 \times 5 = 100$ m^2	$8 \times 5 = 40$ m^2

	H	T	O
	2	0	0
	1	0	0
		8	0
+		4	0
	4	2	0
	1		

The total area of the new supermarket will be 420 m^2.

This is the same as 28×15.

13

Think together

1 This is the floor plan for a new toy shop.

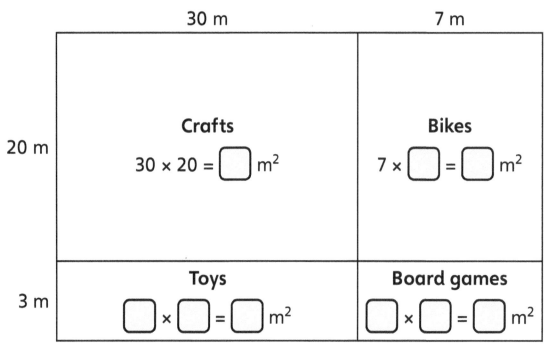

30 m   7 m

20 m

Crafts

30 × 20 = ☐ m²

Bikes

7 × ☐ = ☐ m²

3 m

Toys

☐ × ☐ = ☐ m²

Board games

☐ × ☐ = ☐ m²

a) Find the area of each section in the new toy shop.

b) What is the total area of the new toy shop?

	H	T	O
+			

2 Use the area model to work out 52 × 18.

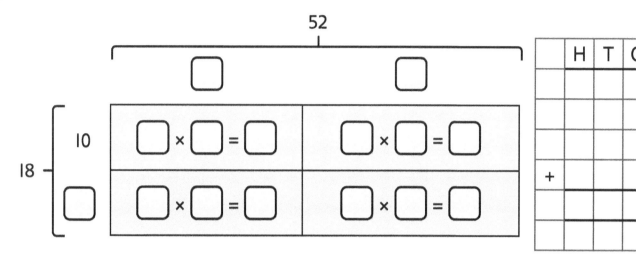

52 × 18 = ☐

3 a) Draw an area model to work out each of these calculations.

CHALLENGE

45 × 37   29 × 81   38²

The boxes in your area models do not need to be exactly to scale. They do need to be big enough to write in the calculations.

b) Max says that the answer to 34 × 18 is 594.

How do you know that Max is not correct just by looking at the last digits in the multiplication?

15

→ **Practice book 5B p9**

Multiply 2-digit numbers

Discover

34×27

Richard

	30	4
20	$30 \times 20 = 600$	$4 \times 20 = 80$
7	$30 \times 7 = 210$	$4 \times 7 = 28$

	Th	H	T	O
		6	0	0
		2	1	0
		8	0	
+		2	8	
	1	8	9	0

Lexi

$34 \times 20 = 680$

			3	4
×				7
		2	3	8
			2	

$680 + 238 = 820$

Zac

			3	4
×			2	7
		2	3	8
	6	8	0	
	9	1	8	

34×7

34×20

34×27

1 **a)** What mistake has Richard made?

b) Look at Lexi's method and Zac's method.

What is the same? What is different?

Share

a) The calculations in the grid are all correct but Richard has lined up the numbers incorrectly in his addition.

	30	4
20	30 × 20 = 600	4 × 20 = 80
7	30 × 7 = 210	4 × 7 = 28

	Th	H	T	O
		6	0	0
		2	1	0
			8	0
+			2	8
		9	1	8
			1	

The correct answer is 918.

b) Lexi partitioned her number and worked out each multiplication separately.

Lexi did that correctly, but she then made a mistake when adding her two totals 680 + 238 = 918.

34 × 20 = 680

		H	T	O
			3	4
×				7
		2	3	8
			2	

Zac did the same as Lexi, except he did it all in one column multiplication and made no mistakes. This is called long multiplication.

		H	T	O	
			3	4	
×			2	7	
		2	3	8	34 × 7
		6	8⟋²0		34 × 20
		9	1	8	34 × 27

Did you notice that Zac placed a 0 here to show that he is multiplying 34 by 20 and not by 2?

17

Think together

1 Mr Jones sets the class some more long multiplication questions.

Complete each multiplication.

a) 46 × 13

	H	T	O
		4	6
×		1	3

46 × 3
46 × 10
46 × 13

c) 37 × 21

	H	T	O
		3	7
×		2	1

37 × 1
37 × 20
37 × 21

b) 34 × 24

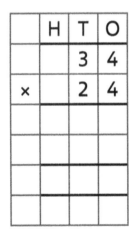

	H	T	O
		3	4
×		2	4

34 × 4
34 × 20
34 × 24

2 Mr Jones's class are going on a school trip.

There are 29 children in the class and they each pay £15.

How much money is paid in total by all the children?

3 **a)** Josh works out 63 × 24.

	Th	H	T	O
			6	3
×			2	4
	2	4	1	2
	1	2	6	0
	3	6	7	2

What mistake has Josh made?

Show the correct long multiplication.

b) Zac has worked out another multiplication.

What two numbers has Zac multiplied together?

	H	T	O
		❄	❄
×		❄	❄
	3	8	7
	4	²3	0
	8	1	7
	₁		

I will think about what two numbers multiply together to make 27 first.

19

→ Practice book 5B p12

Multiply a 3-digit number by a 2-digit number

Discover

These 143 packs are for the local supermarket.

MEGA FLAKES CEREAL

100 packs

40 packs

1 pack

1 pack

1 pack

1 pack = 12 boxes

1 **a)** How many boxes of cereal are there in 143 packs?

Use the grid method to work out the answer.

b) Check your answer using long multiplication.

Share

a) There are 12 boxes of cereal in each pack.

	100	40	3
10	100 × 10 = 1,000	40 × 10 = 400	3 × 10 = 30
2	100 × 2 = 200	40 × 2 = 80	3 × 2 = 6

	Th	H	T	O
	1	0	0	0
		4	0	0
		2	0	0
			8	0
			3	0
+				6
	1	7	1	6
			1	

143 × 12 = 1,716

There are 1,716 boxes of cereal in total.

b) You can extend the method of long multiplication from the last lesson.

	Th	H	T	O	
		1	4	3	
×			1	2	
		2	8	6	143 × 2
	1	4	3	0	143 × 10
	1	7	1	6	143 × 12
			1		

First, I multiplied each digit in the 3-digit number by 2.

Then I multiplied each digit by 10. To do this I put in the 0 and then multiplied each digit by 1.

Finally I added the two calculations together.

143 × 12 = 1,716

So the answer found with the grid method is correct.

Think together

1 Mega Flakes also makes larger packs that each contain 16 boxes of cereal.

A supermarket buys 217 of these packs.

1 pack = 16 boxes

How many boxes of cereal does the supermarket buy in total?

Work it out using the grid method and long multiplication.

Grid method:

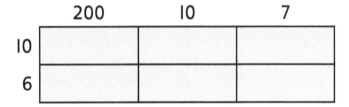

	200	10	7
10			
6			

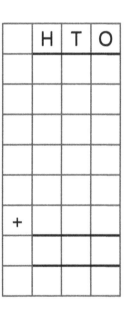

	H	T	O
+			

Long multiplication:

	H	T	O
	2	1	7
×		1	6
			2
		₄	0

217 × 6

217 × 10

2 Complete these multiplications.

a) 263 × 32 = ☐

	H	T	O
	2	6	3
×		3	2

263 × 2
263 × 30
263 × 32

b) 520 × 26 = ☐

	H	T	O
	5	2	0
×		2	6

520 × 6
520 × 20
520 × 26

CHALLENGE

3 Mo has five digit cards.

 1 3 5 7 9

He uses the cards to make a 2-digit number and a 3-digit number and then multiplies them together.

1 5   3 9 7

a) What answer should Mo get?

b) Rearrange the cards to make a multiplication with a bigger answer. Is there a multiplication that gives a smaller answer?

I am just going to try some numbers and see how big an answer I get.

I will write the 3-digit number above the 2-digit number for my multiplications.

23

Multiply a 4-digit number by a 2-digit number

Discover

I **a)** There are 1,274 adults watching the show.

How much money has been made from adult tickets?

b) All the seats have been filled.

How much money has been made from child tickets?

Share

a) An adult ticket costs £32.

1,274 adult tickets were sold.

> I multiplied 1,274 by 32 to find the total amount.

First multiply 1,274 by 2.

	TTh	Th	H	T	O
		1	2	7	4
×				3	2
		2	5	4	8
			1		

1,274 × 2

Then multiply 1,274 by 30.

	TTh	Th	H	T	O
		1	2	7	4
×				3	2
		2	5	4	8
	3	8	2	2	0
		2	1		

1,274 × 2

1,274 × 30

We put down the 0 and multiply each digit by 3.

Finally add up the numbers.

	TTh	Th	H	T	O
		1	2	7	4
×				3	2
		2	5	4	8
	3	8	2	2	0
	4	0	7	6	8
	1				

1,274 × 2

1,274 × 30

1,274 × 32

> I was going to use the grid method, but this seems much quicker.

£40,768 has been made from adult tickets.

b) There are 1,659 people watching the show in total.

1,274 of these people are adults.

1,659	
1,274	385

	Th	H	T	O
	1	⁵6̸	¹5	9
−	1	2	7	4
		3	8	5

There are 385 children watching the show.

A child ticket costs £19.

	Th	H	T	O
		3	8	5
×			1	9
	3	4	6	5
	3	8⁷	5⁴	0
	7	3	1	5
		₁	₁	

£7,315 has been made from child tickets.

Think together

1 Complete these long multiplications.

a) 1,226 × 21

	HTh	TTh	Th	H	T	O
			1	2	2	6
×					2	1

b) 3,405 × 35

	HTh	TTh	Th	H	T	O
			3	4	0	5
×					3	5

2 A plane flies from London to Rome and back again twice a day.

The distance of the flight from London to Rome is 1,445 km.

How far does the plane travel in 25 days?

3 Work out the missing digits.

CHALLENGE

a)

	Th	H	T	O
			7	*
×			1	6
		4	*	0
		7	*	0
	1	*	*	0

b)

	TTh	Th	H	T	O
		*	4	*	9
×				3	6
	*	*	4	5	*
	7	*	*	*	0
	*	*	*	*	4

I need to use the second line of the calculation in **b)** to work out how many thousands are in the top number.

→ Practice book 5B p18

Divide a number up to 4 digits by a 1-digit number ①

Discover

① a) Mr Lopez and Miss Hall share the 64 tickets equally.

How many tickets does each class get?

b) There are 48 children at the fair. They all go on the roller coaster together.

How many cars will they need in total?

Share

a)

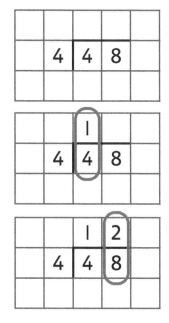

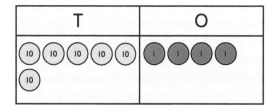

6 tens divided by 2 is 3 tens.
Write 3 in the 10s place.

4 ones divided by 2 is 2 ones.
Write 2 in the 1s place.

64 ÷ 2 = 32

Each class gets 32 tickets.

b)

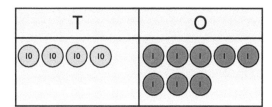

4 tens divided by 4 is 1 ten.
Write 1 in the 10s place.

8 ones divided by 4 is 2 ones.
Write 2 in the 1s place.

48 ÷ 4 = 12

They will need 12 cars in total.

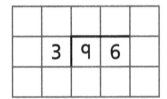

Think together

1 96 pens are shared equally between 3 classes.

How many pens does each class receive?

	3	9	6		

T	O
⑩ ⑩ ⑩ ⑩ ⑩ ⑩ ⑩ ⑩ ⑩	① ① ① ① ① ①

2 Complete these divisions.

a) 428 ÷ 2 = ⬚

	2	4	2	8		

H	T	O
⑩⑩ ⑩⑩ ⑩⑩ ⑩⑩	⑩ ⑩	① ① ① ① ① ① ① ①

b) 9,636 ÷ 3 = ⬚

	3	9	6	3	6	

Th	H	T	O
⑴⑴⑴⑴⑴ ⑴⑴⑴⑴	⑩⑩ ⑩⑩ ⑩⑩ ⑩⑩ ⑩⑩ ⑩⑩	⑩ ⑩ ⑩	① ① ① ① ① ①

CHALLENGE

3 **a)** Over 3 nights, 609 fireworks are set off at the fair. An equal number is set off each night.

The owner of the fair wants to work out how many fireworks were used each night. The owner does this division.

		2	3		
	3	6	0	9	

Is the owner correct? Explain your answer.

I think he is right. I think you just need to put a zero at the end, so he needs **230** fireworks.

Are you sure? I can use multiplication to check if he is correct.

b) Complete these divisions.

9,600 ÷ 3   4,800 ÷ 2   5,055 ÷ 5

31

Divide a number up to 4 digits by a 1-digit number ❷

Discover

1. a) Set out the division that calculates how many pieces of litter each child picked up.

   b) Complete the division.

Share

To work this out, I needed to divide 92 by 4. I used the method of short division that we learnt in the last lesson.

a) 4 children picked up 92 pieces of litter.

They each picked up the same number of pieces.

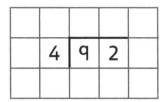 

First, lay out the problem.

b)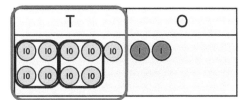

9 tens divided by 4 is 2 remainder 1. Write 2 in the 10s place.

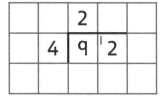 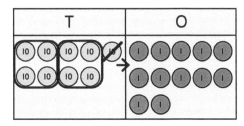

Exchange the remaining 10 for 10 ones. Now there are 12 ones altogether.

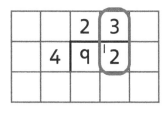 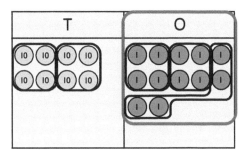

12 ones divided by 4 is 3. Write 3 in the 1s place.

92 ÷ 4 = 23

Think together

1 The children have a flask containing 575 ml of juice.

They share the juice equally among themselves and Mr Jones.

How much juice does each person get?

$575 \div 5 = \boxed{}$ ml

H	T	O
(100) (100) (100) (100) (100)	(10) (10) (10) (10) (10) (10) (10)	(1) (1) (1) (1) (1)

	5	5	7	5

2 Complete these short divisions.

a) $726 \div 6 = \boxed{}$

	6	7	2	6	

H	T	O
(100) (100) (100) (100) (100) (100) (100)	(10) (10)	(1) (1) (1) (1) (1) (1)

b) $522 \div 3 = \boxed{}$

	3	5	2	2	

H	T	O
(100) (100) (100) (100) (100)	(10) (10)	(1) (1)

3 **a)** Look at these division problems.

> There are 312 eggs. How many boxes of 6 eggs can be made?

> Divide 1,980 by 2

> 475 ÷ 5

What is different about these divisions compared with the ones you have been doing so far?

b) Max tries to work out the third division problem. What mistake has Max made?

> I think there is something different in the first step of each division.

		0	3	5	
	5	4	¹7	²5	

c) Complete these divisions.

> 305 ÷ 5

> 615 ÷ 5

> 7,080 ÷ 5

→ Practice book 5B p24

Divide with remainders

Discover

1 a) Count back in 6s from 80 to find the number of full trays that will be filled with cake cases.

b) Calculate 80 ÷ 6 using short division.

Share

a)

$3 \times 6 = 18$ $10 \times 6 = 60$

b)

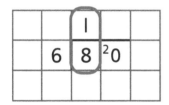

	T	O
	10 10 10 10 10	
	10 10 10	

Layout the division
$80 \div 6$.

	1		
6	8	²0	

	T	O
	10 10 10 10 10	
	10 10 10	

8 tens divided by 6
is 1 remainder 2.

Write 1 in the 10s
place.

Exchange the
remainder 10s.

	1	3	r 2
6	8	²0	

	T	O
	10 10 10	1 1 1 1 1
	10 10 10	1 1 1 1 1
		1 1 1 1 1
		1 1 1 1 1

20 ones divided by
6 is 3 remainder 2.

Write 3 in the 1s
place.

Write r 2.

$80 \div 6 = 13 \text{ r } 2$

37

Think together

1   Lexi wants to share the 80 cakes equally between 3 storage tins.

Will she be able to do this? Discuss your answer with a partner.

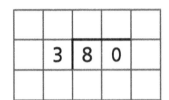

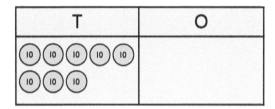

T	O
10 10 10 10 10 10 10 10	

2   Work out these short divisions.

a) $97 \div 7 = \boxed{} \ r \ \boxed{}$

	7	9	7	

T	O
10 10 10 10 10 10 10 10 10	1 1 1 1 1 1 1

b) $173 \div 4 = \boxed{} \ r \ \boxed{}$

	4	1	7	3	

H	T	O
100	10 10 10 10 10 10 10	1 1 1

3 a) Predict which of these divisions will have a remainder.

95 ÷ 5

T	O
10 10 10 10 10 10 10 10 10	● ● ● ● ●

191 ÷ 2

H	T	O
100	10 10 10 10 10 10 10 10 10	●

535 ÷ 4

H	T	O
100 100 100 100 100	10 10 10	● ● ● ● ●

Check using the short division method.

How accurate were your predictions?

b) Is it possible to work out the remainders to these divisions, even though some of the numbers are unknown?

✳6 ÷ 5   7✳3 ÷ 2

✳✳✳6 ÷ 5   73✳ ÷ 2

I think I will use my knowledge of the 2 and 5 times-tables to help me.

39

→ Practice book 5B p27

Efficient division

Discover

I a) 6 slices make one whole pizza.

How do you know that the 253 slices will not make a whole number of pizzas with no spare slices left over?

b) How many whole pizzas can the chefs make?

What fraction of a pizza will be left over?

Share

a) We need to find out if 253 can divide exactly by 6.

1	2	3	4	5	6	7	8	9	10
11	12	13	14	15	16	17	18	19	20
21	22	23	24	25	26	27	28	29	30
31	32	33	34	35	36	37	38	39	40
41	42	43	44	45	46	47	48	49	50
51	52	53	54	55	56	57	58	59	60
61	62	63	64	65	66	67	68	69	70
71	72	73	74	75	76	77	78	79	80
81	82	83	84	85	86	87	88	89	90
91	92	93	94	95	96	97	98	99	100

I marked all the multiples of 6 on a 100 square. I noticed that they are all even numbers.

6 is a multiple of 2 and 3, so a number that is a multiple of 6 is also a multiple of 2 and 3.

253 is not an even number, so it is not a multiple of 2.

253 cannot divide exactly by 6. There will be some slices of pizza left over.

b)

```
      0
  6 2 ²5 3
```

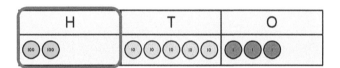

```
    0 4
  6 2 ²5 ¹3
```

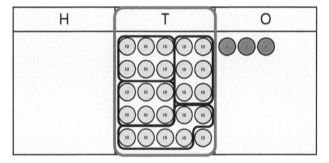

```
    0 4 2 r1
  6 2 ²5 ¹3
```

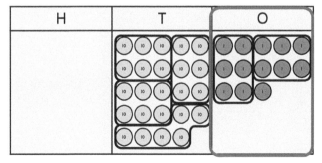

The chefs can make 42 whole pizzas.

There is 1 slice left over. 1 slice is $\frac{1}{6}$ of a pizza.

Think together

1 1,350 grams of flour is divided equally between 5 bowls.

   a) How do you know that 1,350 divides exactly by 5?

   b) How much flour goes into each bowl?

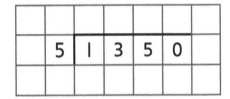

Th		H		T		O
1,000		100 100 100		10 10 10 10 10		

2 What is the remainder in each of these divisions?

575 ÷ 5	137 ÷ 2	140 ÷ 7
576 ÷ 5	138 ÷ 2	142 ÷ 7
577 ÷ 5	139 ÷ 2	45 ÷ 7
579 ÷ 5	140 ÷ 2	1,401 ÷ 7

I wonder if I can work out some of these without doing the division.

3 **a)** Take a copy of the hundred square. Shade in all the multiples of 3.

Pick one of the shaded numbers and add the digits together.

Repeat this two more times.

What do you notice?

1	2	3	4	5	6	7	8	9	10
11	12	13	14	15	16	17	18	19	20
21	22	23	24	25	26	27	28	29	30
31	32	33	34	35	36	37	38	39	40
41	42	43	44	45	46	47	48	49	50
51	52	53	54	55	56	57	58	59	60
61	62	63	64	65	66	67	68	69	70
71	72	73	74	75	76	77	78	79	80
81	82	83	84	85	86	87	88	89	90
91	92	93	94	95	96	97	98	99	100

b) Use this to decide if each of these numbers divides exactly by 3.

729   111   715   1,651   2,538

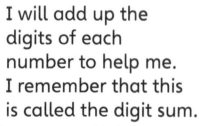

I will add up the digits of each number to help me. I remember that this is called the digit sum.

I think all the digit sums for numbers that divide exactly by 3 are multiples of the same number.

If a number does not divide exactly by 3, how can you work out the remainder without doing the division?

→ Practice book 5B p30

Solve problems with multiplication and division

Discover

Rearrange the digits to make your own 3-digit number.

Now tell me a division fact about your number.

When you divide my number by 4, you get 153 r 3.

5 6 1

My number is a multiple of 6.

Miss Hall

Reena   Kate   Richard   Zac

1   a) What number could Zac have made?

How many possible numbers can you find?

b) What number did Reena make?

Unit 7: Multiplication and division (2), Lesson 10

Share

a)

◯ are multiples of 2.

▢ are multiples of 3.

1	②	3	④	5	⑥	7	⑧	9	⑩
11	⑫	13	⑭	15	⑯	17	⑱	19	⑳
21	㉒	23	㉔	25	㉖	27	㉘	29	㉚
31	㉜	33	㉞	35	㊱	37	㊳	39	㊵
41	㊷	43	㊹	45	㊻	47	㊽	49	㊿
51	52	53	54	55	56	57	58	59	60
61	62	63	64	65	66	67	68	69	70
71	72	73	74	75	76	77	78	79	80
81	82	83	84	85	86	87	88	89	90
91	92	93	94	95	96	97	98	99	100

I saw in a number square that numbers that are multiples of 6 are also multiples of 2 and 3.

The digits 5, 6 and 1 add up to 12, which is a multiple of 3. So, all the numbers that can be made from these digits will be multiples of 3.

Zac's number must also be a multiple of 2, so it will be an even number.

That means his number must end in a 6.

So, there are two numbers that Zac could have made, 516 or 156.

b) We need to find a number that gives an answer of 153 with a remainder of 3, when it is divided by 4.

?

| 153 | 153 | 153 | 153 | 3 |

$612 + 3 = 615$

Reena made the number 615.

	H	T	O
	1	5	3
×			4
	6	1	2
	2	1	

Think together

1 Lexi rearranges these digit cards to make a 3-digit number.

Lexi

When I divide my number by 5, the remainder is 1.

What two numbers could Lexi have made?

2 a) What division calculation is shown here?

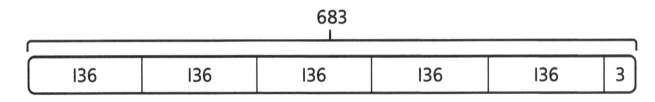

683

| 136 | 136 | 136 | 136 | 136 | 3 |

☐ ÷ ☐ = ☐ r ☐

b) When a 3-digit number is divided by 4, the answer is 47 r 1.

What is the number?

?

3 Richard has these digit cards.

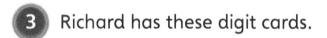

0 1 2 3 4 5 7 9

I made a 3-digit number that I divided by one of the other digits.

My answer has a remainder of 4.

Richard

Write the division that Richard did.

Is there more than one possible division?

I think there are some numbers that you cannot divide by.

I think there are lots of answers. I wonder how many there are altogether.

47

End of unit check

1 What is the missing number in the bar model?

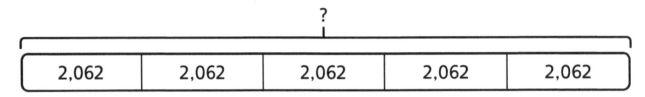

?

| 2,062 | 2,062 | 2,062 | 2,062 | 2,062 |

A 2,062   **B** 10,000   **C** 10,310   **D** 20,620

2 What multiplication is shown using the grid method?

600	80
60	8

A 34 × 22   **B** 20 × 36   **C** 68 × 68   **D** 24 × 32

3 What is the correct first step in the multiplication for 42 × 27?

A

	Th	H	T	O
			4	2
×			2	7
	2	8	1	4

B

		H	T	O
			4	2
×			2	7
			8	4

C

		H	T	O
			4	2
×			2	7
		2	9	4
			1	

D

		H	T	O
			4	2
×			2	7
		1	6	8
			2	

4 Which of these shows the correct answer to 3,892 ÷ 7?

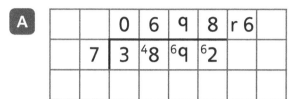

A

		0	6	9	8	r 6	
7	3	⁴8	⁶9	⁶2			

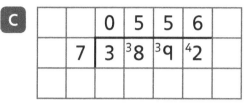

C

		0	5	5	6	
7	3	³8	³9	⁴2		

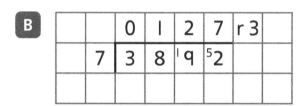

B

		0	1	2	7	r 3	
7	3	8	¹9	⁵2			

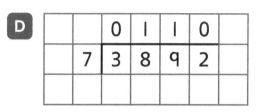

D

		0	1	1	0	
7	3	8	9	2		

5 Aki divides a 3-digit number by 5 and gets a remainder of 4.
What number could Aki have divided?

A 985   B 987   C 989   D 1,004

6 A small car holds 4 people.

How many cars would be needed to take 137 people?

A 34   B 35   C 36   D 141

7 Ebo has a large sack of apples.

If he put them into bags of 4 he would have 72 full bags and
3 apples left over.

If he puts 5 apples into each bag instead, how many bags will he fill?
Will there be any apples left over?

49

→ Practice book 5B p36

Unit 8
Fractions ③

In this unit we will …

⚡ Multiply proper fractions and mixed numbers by whole numbers

⚡ Find a fraction of an amount

⚡ Understand how fractions can be operators

⚡ Solve word problems involving fractions

How can you work out what each part is worth? How many yellow counters are there?

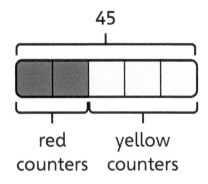

45

red counters   yellow counters

We will need some maths words. Do you know what all of these words mean?

multiply

proper fraction

improper fraction

mixed number

whole(s)

equal parts

divide

fraction of an amount

operator

numerator

denominator

convert

We will also need to represent fractions and mixed numbers using fraction strips. Use this model to work out $2\frac{1}{4} + 2\frac{2}{4}$.

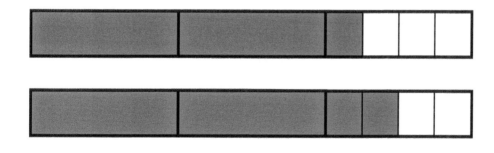

Multiply unit fractions by an integer

Discover

To make I milkshake:

$\frac{1}{5}$ of a jug of milk

10 strawberries

Blend together

① **a)** What fraction of a jug of milk is needed for 3 milkshakes?

b) How many jugs of milk are needed to make 7 milkshakes?

Share

a) For 3 milkshakes, 3 lots of $\frac{1}{5}$ of a jug is needed.

I used addition. The denominators are the same, so I can just add the numerators.

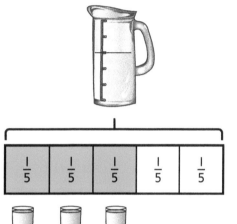

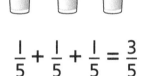

$$\frac{1}{5} + \frac{1}{5} + \frac{1}{5} = \frac{3}{5}$$

I used multiplication.

$$3 \times \frac{1}{5} = \frac{3}{5}$$

Remember that $3 \times \frac{1}{5}$ is the same as $\frac{1}{5} \times 3$.

$\frac{3}{5}$ of the jug of milk is needed to make 3 milkshakes.

b)

I added again.

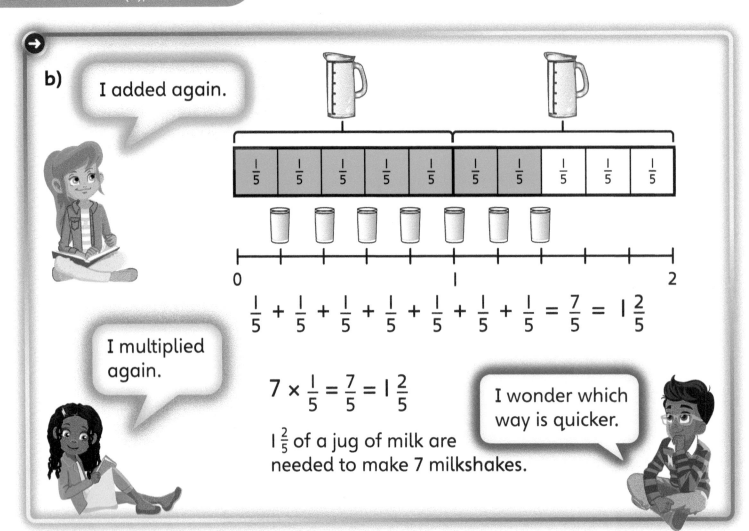

$$\frac{1}{5} + \frac{1}{5} + \frac{1}{5} + \frac{1}{5} + \frac{1}{5} + \frac{1}{5} + \frac{1}{5} = \frac{7}{5} = 1\frac{2}{5}$$

I multiplied again.

$$7 \times \frac{1}{5} = \frac{7}{5} = 1\frac{2}{5}$$

I wonder which way is quicker.

$1\frac{2}{5}$ of a jug of milk are needed to make 7 milkshakes.

Think together

1 A cat eats $\frac{1}{7}$ of a bag of cat food each day.

What fraction of the bag does the cat need for 4 days?

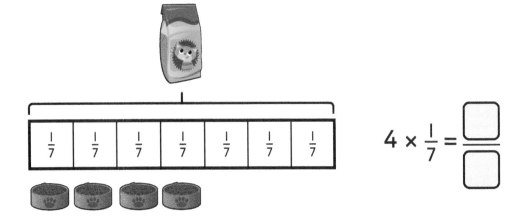

$$4 \times \frac{1}{7} = \frac{\boxed{}}{\boxed{}}$$

2 One glass holds $\frac{1}{8}$ of a bottle of orange juice.

How many bottles do you need for 11 glasses?

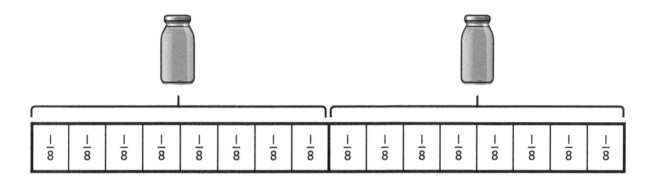

$$\boxed{} \times \dfrac{\boxed{}}{\boxed{}} = \dfrac{\boxed{}}{\boxed{}} = \boxed{} \dfrac{\boxed{}}{\boxed{}}$$

3 **a)** Do all of the following show $\frac{4}{5}$?

$$4 \times \frac{1}{5}$$

$$\frac{1}{5} \times 4$$

$$\frac{1}{5} + \frac{1}{5} + \frac{1}{5} + \frac{1}{5} + \frac{1}{5}$$

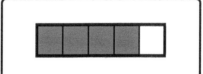

b) Find four ways of showing $\frac{5}{8}$.

→ Practice book 5B p39

Multiply non-unit fractions by an integer

Discover

1 **a)** What fraction of the box is needed each day for the 3 dogs?

b) How many boxes of dog food will Lexi and her mum need to buy to feed the dogs for 5 days?

Share

a) Each dog needs $\frac{2}{9}$ of the box. There are 3 dogs.

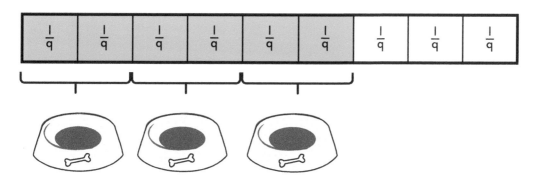

Using addition: $\quad \frac{2}{9} + \frac{2}{9} + \frac{2}{9} = \frac{6}{9} = \frac{2}{3}$

Using multiplication: $\quad \frac{2}{9} \times 3 = \frac{6}{9} = \frac{2}{3}$

$\frac{2}{3}$ of the box is needed each day for the 3 dogs.

b) Each day the dogs need $\frac{2}{3}$ of a box.

There are 5 days.

> I think it is simpler to multiply. To work out how many $\frac{1}{3}$s, I worked out $2 \times 5 = 10$.

$\frac{2}{3} \times 5 = \frac{10}{3} = 3\frac{1}{3}$

The dogs need $3\frac{1}{3}$ boxes for 5 days. Lexi and her mum will need to buy 4 boxes to feed the dogs for 5 days.

Think together

  a) Lexi and her mum each eat $\frac{3}{7}$ of a bar of chocolate.

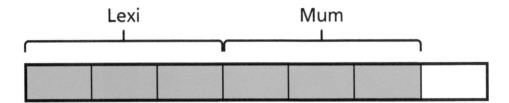

What fraction of the chocolate bar do they eat in total?

$$\frac{3}{7} \times 2 = \frac{\boxed{}}{7}$$

b) A bowl contains $\frac{2}{5}$ l of water.

How much water is there in 3 bowls?

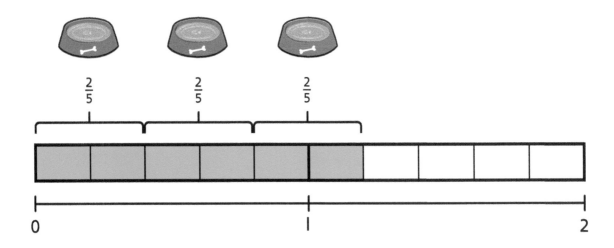

$$\frac{2}{5} \times \boxed{} = \frac{\boxed{}}{\boxed{}} = \boxed{}\frac{\boxed{}}{\boxed{}}$$

2 Kate runs around a circular track.

One lap is $\frac{3}{10}$ of a kilometre.

Kate runs 5 laps. How far does Kate run?

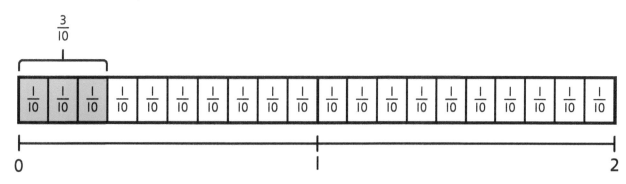

3 Work out the answers to each of the following questions.

Set A	Set B	Set C
$\frac{1}{5} \times 2$	$1 \times \frac{3}{8}$	$\frac{3}{4} \times 4$
$\frac{2}{5} \times 2$	$2 \times \frac{3}{8}$	$\frac{2}{5} \times 5$
$\frac{3}{5} \times 2$	$3 \times \frac{3}{8}$	$\frac{5}{6} \times 6$
$\frac{4}{5} \times 2$	$5 \times \frac{3}{8}$	$7 \times \frac{3}{7}$

Explain your method to a partner.

What do you notice about the answers to Set C?

I have found a way to answer these questions without drawing a diagram each time.

59

→ Practice book 5B p42

Multiply mixed numbers by integers ①

Discover

① **a)** How far does the glacier travel in 3 days?

b) How many days will it take the glacier to travel more than 15 yards?

Share

a) The glacier moves $1\frac{3}{4}$ yards each day.

Multiply $1\frac{3}{4}$ by 3 to work out how far it moves in 3 days.

day 1

day 2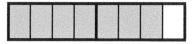

> I converted $1\frac{3}{4}$ to an improper fraction. I then multiplied by 3.

day 3

$1\frac{3}{4} = \frac{7}{4}$

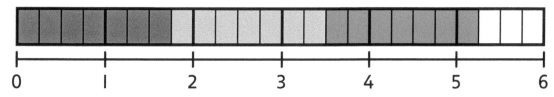

$\frac{7}{4} \times 3 = \frac{21}{4} = 5\frac{1}{4}$

The glacier travels $5\frac{1}{4}$ yards in 3 days.

b) Multiply $\frac{7}{4}$ by different numbers until the answer is greater than 15.

> I used trial and error to find the correct answer.

$\frac{7}{4} \times 6 = \frac{42}{4} = 10\frac{2}{4}$

$\frac{7}{4} \times 7 = \frac{49}{4} = 12\frac{1}{4}$

$\frac{7}{4} \times 8 = \frac{56}{4} = 14$

$\frac{7}{4} \times 9 = \frac{63}{4} = 15\frac{3}{4}$

After 9 days, the glacier has moved more than 15 yards.

A different method:

I compared fractions to work out what I needed to multiply by.

How many $\frac{1}{4}$s in 15 yards? $15 \times 4 = 60$

So, 15 yards is the same as 60 quarters or $\frac{60}{4}$ yards.

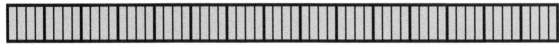

Every day, the glacier travels $\frac{7}{4}$ yards.

$$\frac{7}{4} \times ? > 15 \qquad = \qquad \frac{7}{4} \times ? > \frac{60}{4}$$

The missing number must be 9, because 7×9 is 63 and this is the first number in the 7 times-table that is greater than 60.

After 9 days, the glacier has moved more than 15 yards.

Think together

1 Olivia runs $2\frac{1}{3}$ km every hour. How far does she run in 4 hours?

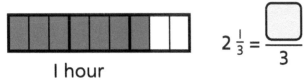

$2\frac{1}{3} = \dfrac{\boxed{}}{3}$

I hour

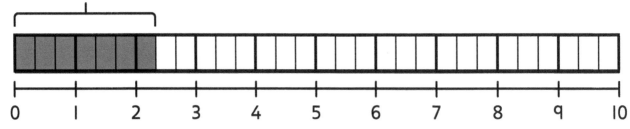

$$\frac{\boxed{}}{3} \times 4 = \frac{\boxed{}}{3} = \boxed{}\frac{\boxed{}}{3}$$

2 **a)** Jamilla has worked out $1\frac{3}{5} \times 4$.

Explain Jamilla's method to a partner. You can use diagrams to help you explain, if necessary.

$$1\frac{3}{5} \times 4$$

$$1\frac{3}{5} = \frac{8}{5}$$

$$\frac{8}{5} \times 4 = \frac{32}{5}$$

$$\frac{32}{5} = 6\frac{2}{5}$$

b) Use Jamilla's method to work out $3\frac{1}{2} \times 5$ and $9 \times 1\frac{1}{10}$.

3 Here are some fractions and whole numbers.

| $1\frac{1}{3}$ | $2\frac{1}{3}$ | $3\frac{2}{3}$ | $3\frac{1}{4}$ |

| 3 | 6 | 9 | 12 |

Multiply each of the fractions in the top row by each number in the bottom row.

Do you notice any patterns?

You can use the method from this lesson or the last lesson to help you.

63

→ Practice book 5B p45

Multiply mixed numbers by integers ❷

Discover

Soup Challenge

For one pot of soup:

$1\frac{1}{6}$ jugs of stock

$1\frac{1}{2}$ onions

$3\frac{1}{4}$ potatoes

1   **a)** 5 children take part in the Soup Challenge.

How many jugs of stock do the children use in total?

b) How many onions do the children use in total?

Share

a) 5 children use $1\frac{1}{6}$ jugs of stock each.

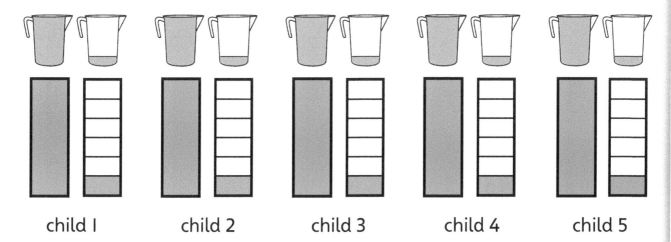

child 1   child 2   child 3   child 4   child 5

> I multiplied the wholes first, then the fractions. Then I added the answers together to find the total.

Multiply the wholes:

$1 \times 5 = 5$

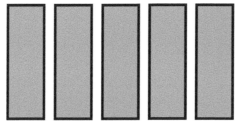

Multiply the parts:

$\frac{1}{6} \times 5 = \frac{5}{6}$

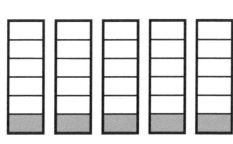

Add to find the total: $5 + \frac{5}{6} = 5\frac{5}{6}$

The children use $5\frac{5}{6}$ jugs of stock in total.

b) Each child needs $1\frac{1}{2}$ onions.

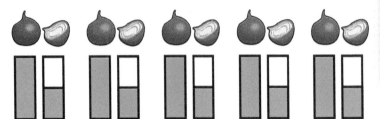

I converted the improper fraction into a mixed number to make it easier to add.

Multiply the wholes: $1 \times 5 = 5$

Multiply the parts: $\frac{1}{2} \times 5 = \frac{5}{2} = 2\frac{1}{2}$

Add together: $5 + 2\frac{1}{2} = 7\frac{1}{2}$

The children use $7\frac{1}{2}$ onions in total.

Think together

I'm going to multiply the wholes and then the parts and add together.

1 Each child also needs $3\frac{1}{4}$ potatoes. How many potatoes are needed in total?

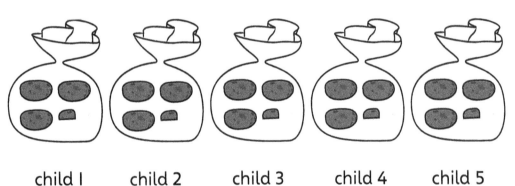

child 1   child 2   child 3   child 4   child 5

2 **a)** Work out $1\frac{2}{5} \times 4$.

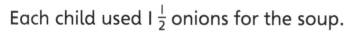

b) Explain how you can use your answer to work out these multiplications.

$2\frac{2}{5} \times 4$ $1\frac{2}{5} \times 5$

3 Mrs Dean gave 4 onions to each of the 5 children.

Each child used $1\frac{1}{2}$ onions for the soup.

How many onions are left over in total?

I will use my answer from earlier and subtract.

I will work out how many one child has left over and then multiply by 5.

67

→ Practice book 5B p48

Fraction of an amount

Discover

1 **a)** There are 320 people in the theme park.

$\frac{2}{5}$ of the people are adults.

How many children are in the theme park?

b) A child ticket is $\frac{3}{8}$ of the cost of an adult ticket.

How much does a child ticket cost?

Share

a) There are 320 people in the theme park.

$\frac{2}{5}$ of the people are adults.

This means $\frac{3}{5}$ of the people are children.

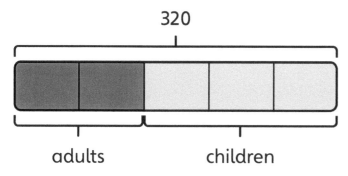

Work out the value of $\frac{1}{5}$ by dividing 320 by 5.

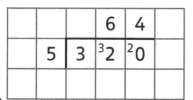

$320 \div 5 = 64$

I drew a bar model to help me represent the situation. 2 parts represent the adults and 3 parts represent the children.

$\frac{3}{5}$ of the people are children, so I multiplied by 3 to work out $\frac{3}{5}$.

I worked out the number of adults and subtracted it from 320. You did it using a more efficient method.

To work out the number of children multiply by 3.

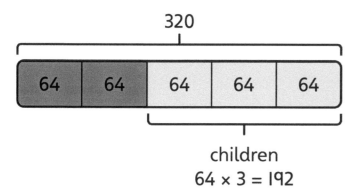

children

$64 \times 3 = 192$

There are 192 children in the theme park.

b) A child ticket costs $\frac{3}{8}$ of an adult ticket.

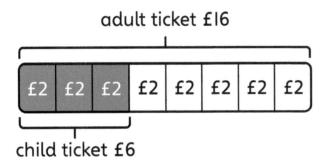

Find out the value of $\frac{1}{8}$ by dividing the adult ticket cost by 8:   £16 ÷ 8 = £2

To find the cost of a child ticket, multiply by 3:   £2 × 3 = £6

A child ticket costs £6.

Think together

1 There are 78 people on the roller coaster.

$\frac{1}{6}$ of the people are under 16 years old.

How many people are 16 years or over?

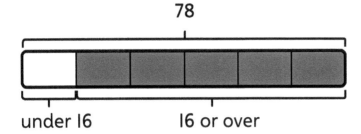

2 Luis spends $\frac{7}{10}$ of his time at the theme park in queues.

Luis spends 210 minutes in the theme park.

How long does he spend queuing?

3 The pictogram shows the ratings for the theme park on the internet.

5 stars	😃 😃 😃
4 stars	😃 😃 😃 😃 😃 😃 😃 😃
3 stars	😃 😃 😃 😃 😃
2 stars	😃 😃 😃
I star	😃

1,680 people have rated the theme park in total.

How many people gave the theme park 2 stars or less?

I worked out what one symbol represents by dividing, and then I multiplied.

I think that those who gave '2 stars or less' means those who gave 2 stars **and** those who gave I star.

71

Finding the whole

Discover

There is $\frac{1}{3}$ of the jar left.

Reena

1 **a)** There is 200 g of jam left in the jar.

How many grams of jam are in the jar when it is full?

b) Reena eats 60 g of cheese.

$\frac{3}{5}$ of the block of cheese is left.

How many grams of cheese are left?

Share

a) There are 200 g of jam left in the jar.

I knew there are 3 lots of this amount in a full jar.

200 g × 3 = 600 g

There are 600 g of jam in the jar when it is full.

b) $\frac{3}{5}$ of the block of cheese is left.

This means that Reena has eaten $\frac{2}{5}$ of the block.

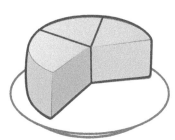

I knew that 2 parts represent 60 g of cheese.

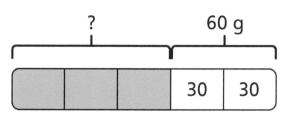

60 ÷ 2 = 30

30 × 3 = 90

There are 90 g of cheese left.

Think together

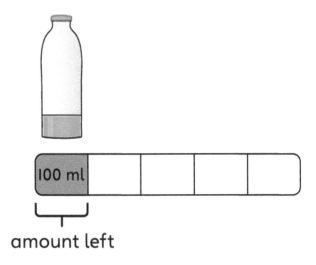

1 Rebecca has a bottle of juice.

There is $\frac{1}{5}$ left in the bottle.

There are 100 ml left.

amount left

How much juice was in the bottle when it was full?

> I know $1 - \frac{2}{7} = \frac{5}{7}$.
> I will use this information to help me work out the answer.

2 Erik eats $\frac{2}{7}$ of a packet of sweets.

There are 35 sweets left in the packet.

How many sweets were in it when it was full?

74

3 Lexi and Andy each have a box of chocolates.

Who had more chocolates in their box to start with?

I have eaten $\frac{3}{7}$ of my chocolates.

I have eaten $\frac{5}{8}$ of my chocolates.

Lexi

Andy

28 chocolates left   15 chocolates left

28

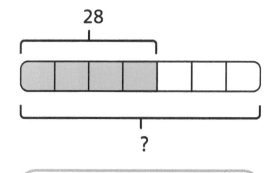

Lexi's chocolate box

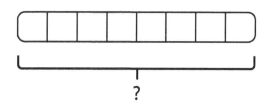

Andy's chocolate box

I wonder how many sevenths Lexi's **28** chocolates represent.

I am going to work out what fraction of the box Andy has left.

75

→ **Practice book 5B p54**

Using fractions as operators

Discover

Amal

Toshi

1 **a)** Who has painted $\frac{1}{3}$ of 6?

Who has painted $\frac{1}{3} \times 6$?

b) Who has painted the greater amount of the fence?

What is the same and what is different about these calculations?

Share

a) Amal has painted 2 out of 6 panels.

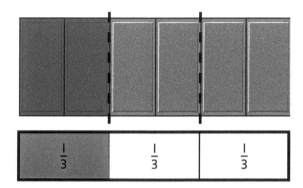

$\frac{2}{6} = \frac{1}{3}$

Amal has painted $\frac{1}{3}$ of 6.

Toshi has painted $\frac{1}{3}$ of each of the 6 panels.

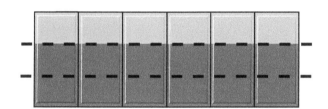

Toshi has painted $\frac{1}{3} \times 6$.

I recognised that the answers are the same, so $\frac{1}{3}$ of 6 is the same as saying $\frac{1}{3} \times 6$.

b)

Amal's fence

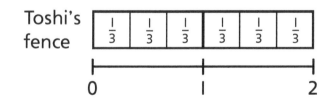

$6 \div 3 = 2$

So $\frac{1}{3}$ of $6 = 2$

Toshi's fence

$\frac{1}{3} \times 6 = \frac{6}{3}$

$\frac{6}{3} = 2$

They have both painted the same amount of the fence.

One calculation involves dividing 6 into 3, the other involves multiplying $\frac{1}{3}$ by 6.

Think together

1 **a)** Work out $\frac{2}{5}$ of 15.

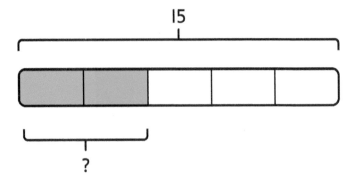

$\frac{1}{5}$ of 15 is ☐ so, $\frac{2}{5}$ of 15 is ☐.

b) Calculate 15 lots of $\frac{2}{5}$.

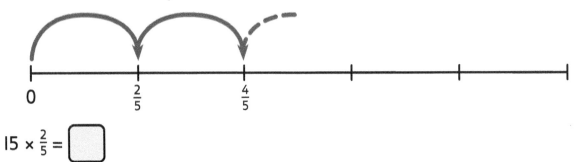

$15 \times \frac{2}{5} = $ ☐

c) What do you notice about your answers to parts **a)** and **b)**?

2 Which calculations will give the same answer?

$\frac{1}{10} \times 120$	$84 \times \frac{2}{3}$	$\frac{2}{3}$ of 84
$\frac{3}{4}$ of 24	$\frac{3}{4} \times 24$	$\frac{1}{10}$ of 120

3 Olivia and Mo are working out some calculations.

a) Olivia is working out $\frac{3}{4} \times 24$.

Olivia

I can think of this as being the same as $\frac{3}{4}$ of 24.

Use Olivia's method to work out $\frac{3}{4} \times 24$.

b) Mo is working out $\frac{1}{3}$ of 7.

Mo

I can think of this as being the same as $\frac{1}{3} \times 7$.

Use Mo's method to work out $\frac{1}{3}$ of 7.

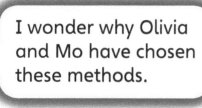

I wonder why Olivia and Mo have chosen these methods.

I think they have chosen the most efficient way of working out their calculation.

79

End of unit check

1 What is $\frac{1}{8} \times 3$?

A $\frac{3}{8}$ **B** $\frac{1}{24}$ **C** 24   **D** $\frac{3}{24}$

2 What is the missing number?

$\frac{2}{9} \times 5 = \frac{1}{9} \times \boxed{}$

A $\frac{10}{9}$ **B** $\frac{5}{9}$ **C** 10   **D** 5

3 A bag contains $1\frac{1}{4}$ kg of potatoes.

What is the total weight of 5 bags of potatoes?

A $\frac{5}{4}$ **B** $5\frac{1}{4}$ **C** 6   **D** $6\frac{1}{4}$

4 A box contains red and yellow counters.

There are 72 counters in the box.

$\frac{3}{8}$ of the counters are red.

How many yellow counters are in the box?

A $\frac{5}{8}$ B 45   C 27   D 72

5 Complete the statement.

$\frac{1}{3} \times 5 = \frac{1}{3}$ of ☐

A $\frac{5}{3}$ B $1\frac{2}{3}$ C $\frac{5}{9}$ D 5

6 What is $3 \times 1\frac{3}{4}$?

A $3\frac{3}{4}$ B $\frac{9}{4}$ C $5\frac{1}{4}$ D $4\frac{1}{4}$

7 In the morning Lee eats $\frac{5}{6}$ of a packet of nuts.

In the afternoon he eats $\frac{1}{2}$ of what is left.

The bag contained 144 nuts.

How many nuts does he have left?

8 $\frac{2}{3}$ of a number is 18.

What is $\frac{5}{9}$ of the number?

→ Practice book 5B p60

Unit 9
Decimals and percentages

In this unit we will ...

⚡ Read and write decimals up to three decimal places, including numbers greater than 1

⚡ Round decimals to nearest whole number and to one decimal place

⚡ Order and compare decimal numbers up to three decimal places

⚡ Write percentages as fractions and as decimals

Do you remember what this is called? We use it to understand the place value of digits in a number.

How would you place 0·034 into the grid?

O	Tth	Hth	Thths

We will need some maths words. Do you know what they all mean?

decimal   decimal place   tenths

hundredths   thousandths   decimal point

place value   digits   fractions

per cent (%)   percentage

We need to use a number line too. Use it to help you show equivalent fractions, decimals and percentages.

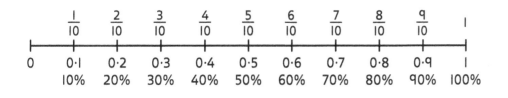

| $\frac{1}{10}$ | $\frac{2}{10}$ | $\frac{3}{10}$ | $\frac{4}{10}$ | $\frac{5}{10}$ | $\frac{6}{10}$ | $\frac{7}{10}$ | $\frac{8}{10}$ | $\frac{9}{10}$ | 1 |

| 0 | 0·1 | 0·2 | 0·3 | 0·4 | 0·5 | 0·6 | 0·7 | 0·8 | 0·9 | 1 |
| | 10% | 20% | 30% | 40% | 50% | 60% | 70% | 80% | 90% | 100% |

Write decimals up to 2 decimal places – less than 1

Discover

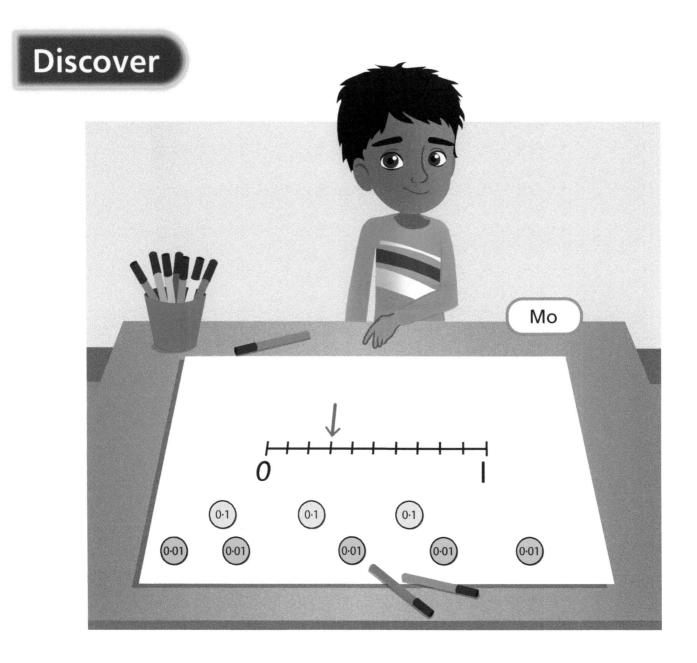

1 **a)** What number is the arrow pointing to?

b) What number has Mo made using counters?

Share

a) This number line counts up in tenths. The arrow points to 0·3.

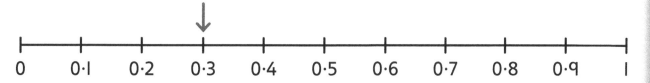

0   0·1   0·2   0·3   0·4   0·5   0·6   0·7   0·8   0·9   1

b) Put the counters into a place value grid.

O		Tth	Hth
	•	0·1 0·1 0·1	0·01 0·01 0·01 0·01 0·01
0	•	3	5

Mo has made the number 0·35.

I remember how to read decimal numbers.

We do not say 'zero point thirty-five'. We say each number after the decimal point separately. So we say 'zero point three five'.

Think together

1   What numbers are shown on these number lines?

a)
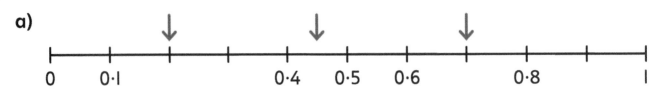

b)
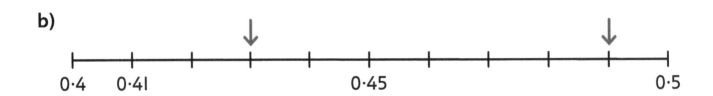

2   What numbers are shown?

a)
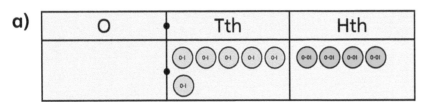

b)
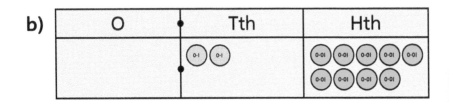

I will read the
numbers out loud.

c) 0·1   0·01 0·01 0·01 0·01 0·01

3 Malik has made this number.

O	•	Tth	Hth
		0·1 0·1 0·1 0·1	0·01 0·01 0·01 0·01 0·01

a) What number has Malik made?

b) What is the value of each of the digits in Malik's number?

c) Malik adds these counters to his grid.

0·1   0·1   0·1

What number has Malik got now?

d) Where would Malik's number be on the number line?

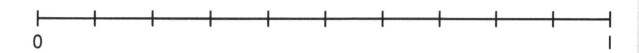

0   1

I will make the number on a place value grid.

I think Malik's decimal on the number line is exactly half-way between two of the points.

87

→ Practice book 5B p62

Write decimals up to 2 decimal places – greater than 1

Discover

Richard · Isla · Bella

1 **a)** What is Isla's score?

b) Bella scores 1·45.

Represent this number using counters on a place value grid.

What is the value of each of the digits in the number?

Share

a) Isla's score is between 1 and 2.

I counted each interval on the number line.

The scale is divided into tenths. Isla's score is 1·4.

b) Bella's score is 1·45. This is half-way between 1·4 and 1·5.

O		Tth	Hth
1		0·1 0·1 0·1 0·1	0·01 0·01 0·01 0·01 0·01

1 represents 1 one (or 1).

4 represents 4 tenths (or 0·4).

5 represents 5 hundredths (or 0·05).

The position of each digit in the place value grid helped me work out its value.

Think together

1 What number has each child scored?

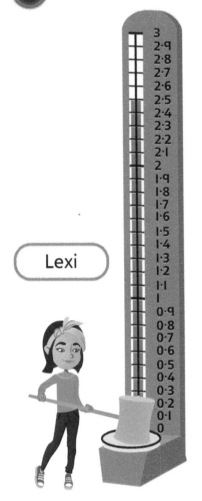

Lexi

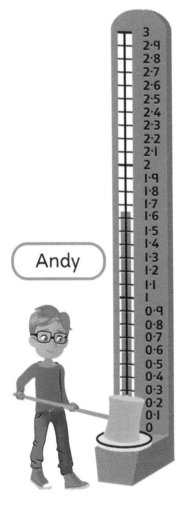

Andy

Lee

2 What numbers are represented here?

a)

O		Tth	Hth
		0·1 0·1 0·1 0·1 0·1	
		0·1 0·1	

b)

O		Tth	Hth
1 1 1			0·01 0·01 0·01 0·01 0·01

I wonder what happens if there are no counters in the tenths column, but there are in the hundredths column.

90

3 Ebo and Kate are counting in tenths.
Explain and correct their mistakes.

a)

1·6, 1·7, 1·8, 1·9. 1·10, 1·11

Ebo

b)

2·3, 2·2, 2·1, 2·09, 2·08, 2·07

Kate

I can show the mistakes using place value counters and exchange.

I will show the mistakes by writing the numbers in a place value grid.

91

→ Practice book 5B p65

Equivalent fractions and decimals – tenths

Discover

Sofia

Distance run
0·5 km

Route planner
0 1 2 3

1 **a)** Where is Sofia on the route planner? Find the location on the route planner, and describe it as a fraction of a kilometre.

b) After 15 minutes Sofia has run 1·5 km. Locate her position on the route planner, and describe it as a fraction of a kilometre.

Share

a) 0·5 is equivalent to one half.

0·5 is equivalent to a half, because five tenths is half-way between zero tenths and ten tenths.

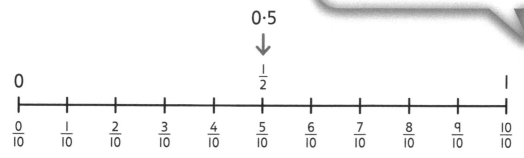

I think you could also write her distance as $\frac{5}{10}$ km, because $\frac{5}{10}$ is equivalent to $\frac{1}{2}$.

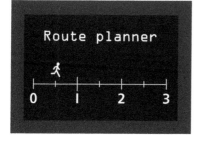

O		Tth
0	•	5

Sofia has run 0·5 km, which can also be written as $\frac{1}{2}$ km.

b)

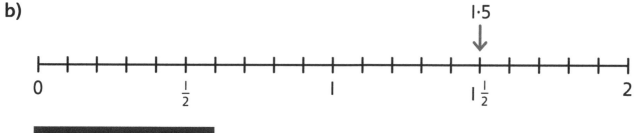

O		Tth
1	•	5

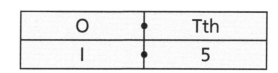

1·5 is equivalent to $1\frac{1}{2}$ and $1\frac{5}{10}$.

93

Think together

 a) Jamie ran 0·7 km.

Represent this on a place value grid using counters.

O		Tth

b) Write 0·7 as a fraction.

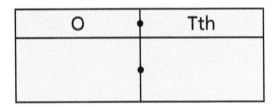

2 These are the results for some other runners. Complete the table.

Runner	Distance as a decimal	Distance as a fraction
Aki	0·6 km	☐ km
Richard	☐ km	$\frac{3}{10}$ km
Jamilla	☐ km	$\frac{9}{10}$ km
Ambika	☐ km	$2\frac{3}{10}$ km

3 Here are some fraction and decimal cards.

Sort them into two groups. In each group you should have an equivalent improper fraction, a mixed number and a decimal.

$\frac{35}{10}$

$2\frac{3}{10}$

3·5

$3\frac{1}{2}$

$\frac{23}{10}$

2·3

I'm not sure if $3\frac{1}{2}$ is equivalent to anything.

I think you can write $3\frac{1}{2}$ as 3 and some tenths.

95

Equivalent fractions and decimals – hundredths

Discover

1 **a)** Write the memory required for the games app as a fraction.

b) Write the memory required for the music app as a fraction in two different ways. Explain your answer.

Share

a) The games app requires 0·08 GB.

O		Tth	Hth
			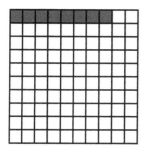

I showed this on a place value grid and a hundredths grid.

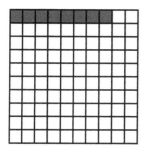 0·08 is equivalent to $\frac{8}{100}$. 0·08 GB = $\frac{8}{100}$ GB.

b) The music app requires 0·10 GB.

0·10 is equivalent to $\frac{10}{100}$ or $\frac{1}{10}$ GB.

I understood that both $\frac{10}{100}$ and $\frac{1}{10}$ = 0·10 by thinking about exchange.

10 hundredths   1 tenth

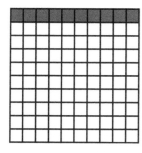 

O		Tth	Hth
		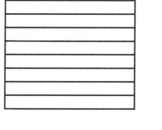	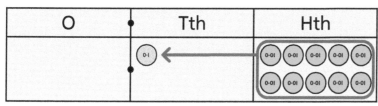

You can write 0·10 as $\frac{1}{10}$ or $\frac{10}{100}$.

Think together

  a) A reading app requires 0·15 GB of memory. Write this as a fraction.

O		Tth	Hth
	0·1		0·01 0·01 0·01 0·01 0·01

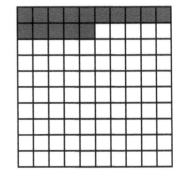

$$0.15 \text{ GB} = \frac{\Box}{\Box} \text{ GB}$$

> There is often more than one way to write a fraction.

b) Bella's computer has $\frac{17}{100}$ GB memory remaining. Write this as a decimal.

O		Tth	Hth
			0·01 0·01 0·01 0·01 0·01
			0·01 0·01 0·01 0·01 0·01
			0·01 0·01 0·01 0·01 0·01
			0·01 0·01

$$\frac{17}{100} \text{ GB} = \boxed{} \text{ GB}$$

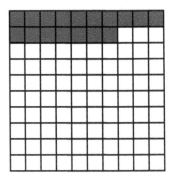

2 Write each number as a decimal and as a fraction.

a)

O	Tth	Hth
	0·1 0·1	0·01 0·01 0·01

b)

O	Tth	Hth
1	0·1	0·01 0·01 0·01 0·01 0·01
		0·01 0·01 0·01 0·01

c)

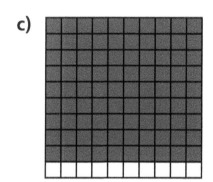

3 Write each of these decimals as both improper fractions and as mixed numbers.

The first one has been done for you.

a) 1·27 is equivalent to $\frac{127}{100}$ and $1\frac{27}{100}$.

b) 2·32

c) 2·20

d) 1·05

I remember that I can write 1 whole as $\frac{100}{100}$.

e) 3·5

→ Practice book 5B p71

Equivalent fractions and decimals

Discover

Jamie

Luis

1 **a)** What fraction of their grid has each child covered?

b) Write each fraction as a decimal.

Share

a) Each peg board is made up of 100 holes.

Jamie has put pegs in 20 holes.

Jamie has covered $\frac{2}{10}$ of her grid or $\frac{1}{5}$.

Luis has covered 25 squares.

This is the same as $\frac{1}{4}$ of the grid.

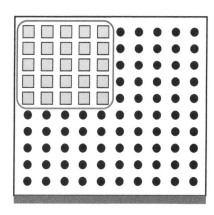

b) $\frac{2}{10}$ and $\frac{1}{5}$ are equal to 0·2.

$\frac{1}{4}$ is equal to 0·25.

I know from the last lesson that $\frac{2}{10}$ is equal to 0·2. So $\frac{1}{5}$ must also equal 0·2.

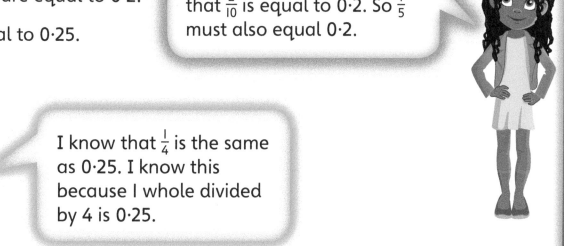

I know that $\frac{1}{4}$ is the same as 0·25. I know this because I whole divided by 4 is 0·25.

Think together

1 Write each number represented as a fraction and decimal.

a)

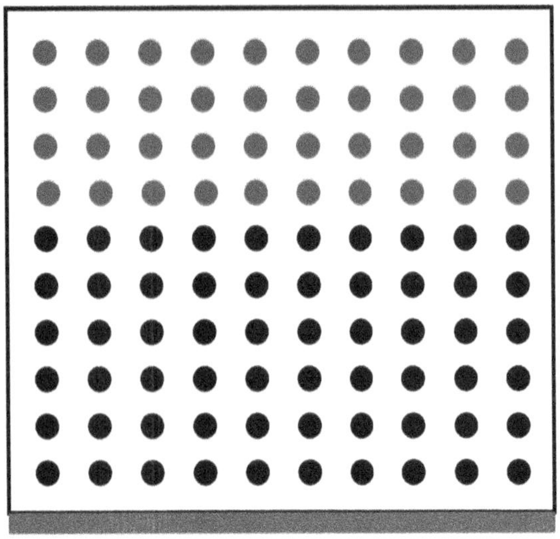

b)

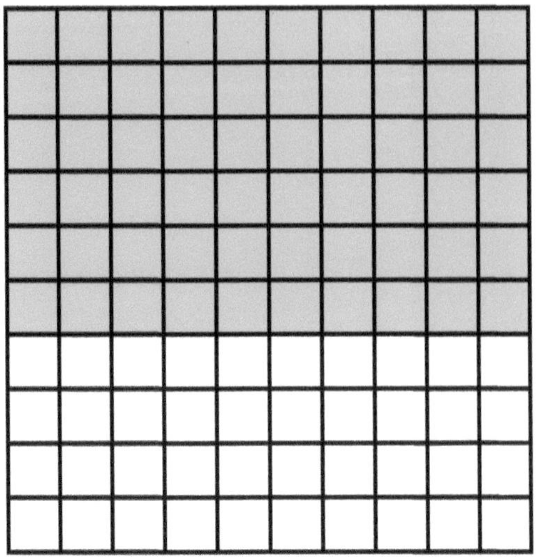

2 Complete the table.

Fraction	Decimal
$\frac{4}{5}$	
	0·5
	0·75
$1\frac{2}{5}$	
$2\frac{1}{4}$	

 Work out where each fraction goes on the number line.

$\frac{1}{5}$ $\frac{3}{5}$ $\frac{4}{5}$ $\frac{1}{4}$ and $\frac{3}{4}$

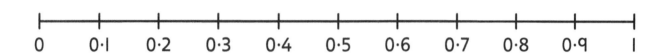

This line goes up in decimals, but the cards are fractions.

I think we need to find equivalents to help us.

103

Thousandths as fractions

Discover

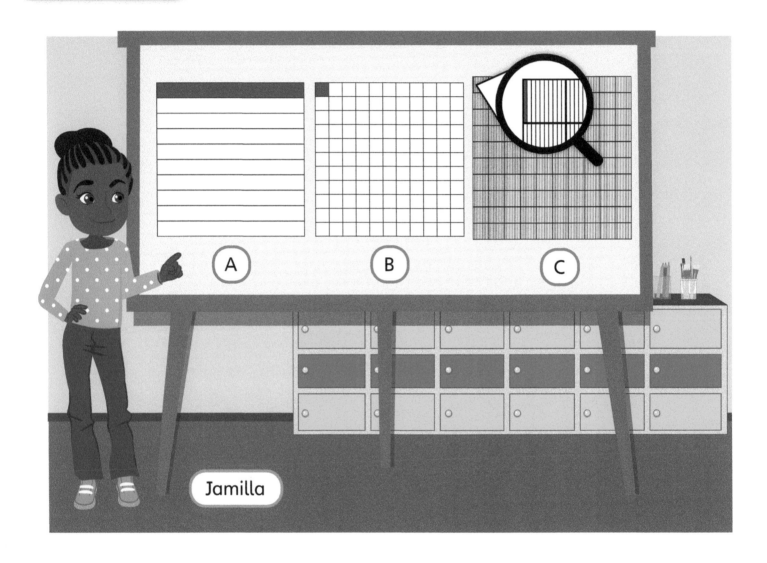

Jamilla

1 **a)** What fraction and decimal of grids A and B have been shaded?

b) What fraction of grid C has been shaded?

Share

a) Each grid represents a whole.

   (A) The whole is split into 10 equal parts.

      Each part is $\frac{1}{10}$.

      $\frac{1}{10} = 0 \cdot 1$

   (B) Now each tenth is split into 10 equal parts. There are 100 equal parts.

      Each part is $\frac{1}{100}$.

      $\frac{1}{100} = 0 \cdot 01$

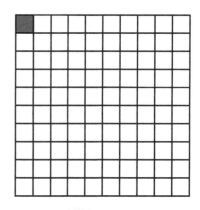

b) **(C)** Now each hundredth is split into 10 equal parts. There are 1,000 equal parts.

      Each part is $\frac{1}{1,000}$.

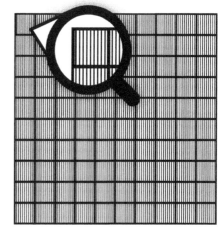

$\frac{1}{1,000}$ is a thousandth.

Think together

1 Write each shaded area as a fraction.

a)

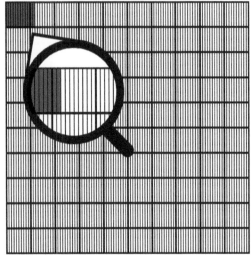

$$\frac{\boxed{}}{1,000}$$

b)

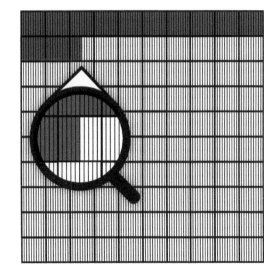

$$\frac{\boxed{}}{1,000}$$

c)

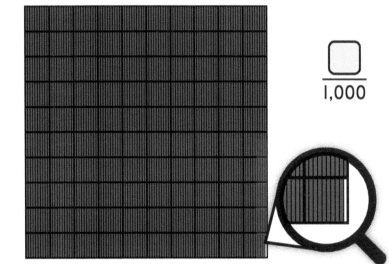

$$\frac{\boxed{}}{1,000}$$

2 Write each of these numbers as a fraction.

a)

$\frac{1}{1,000}$ $\frac{1}{1,000}$ $\frac{1}{1,000}$ $\frac{1}{1,000}$ $\frac{1}{1,000}$

$\frac{1}{1,000}$ $\frac{1}{1,000}$ $\frac{1}{1,000}$ $\frac{1}{1,000}$

b)

$\frac{1}{1,000}$ $\frac{1}{1,000}$ $\frac{1}{1,000}$ $\frac{1}{1,000}$ $\frac{1}{1,000}$

$\frac{1}{1,000}$ $\frac{1}{1,000}$ $\frac{1}{1,000}$ $\frac{1}{1,000}$ $\frac{1}{1,000}$

$\frac{1}{1,000}$ $\frac{1}{1,000}$ $\frac{1}{1,000}$ $\frac{1}{1,000}$ $\frac{1}{1,000}$

$\frac{1}{1,000}$ $\frac{1}{1,000}$ $\frac{1}{1,000}$ $\frac{1}{1,000}$ $\frac{1}{1,000}$

c)

$\frac{1}{100}$ $\frac{1}{1,000}$ $\frac{1}{1,000}$

I wonder if I will need to do an exchange.

3 How many thousandths are equivalent to:

a) $\frac{1}{2}$

b) $\frac{1}{4}$

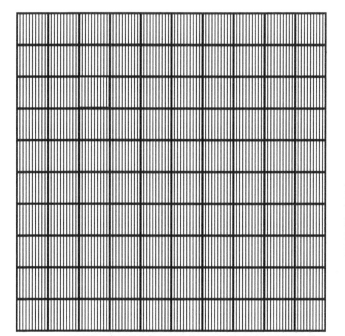

I need to think what part of the grid will be shaded.

I know that this grid is split into 1,000 equal parts.

CHALLENGE

→ Practice book 5B p77

Thousandths as decimals

Discover

Reena

1 **a)** What fraction of the grid has Reena shaded?

b) Write the fraction as a decimal.

Share

a)

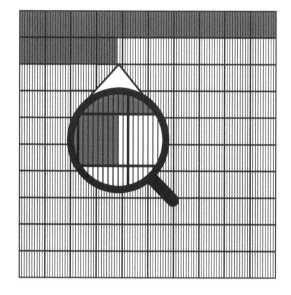

Reena has shaded in $\frac{138}{1,000}$.

b)

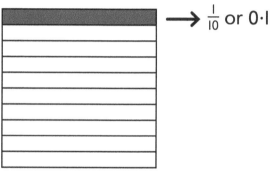 → $\frac{1}{10}$ or 0·1

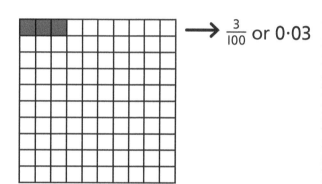 → $\frac{3}{100}$ or 0·03

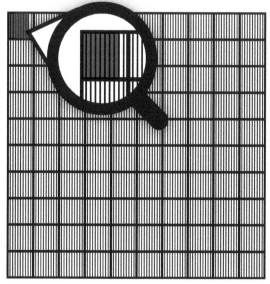

→ $\frac{8}{1,000}$ or 0·008

I saw how to get 0·138 from 0·1, 0·03 and 0·008.

$\frac{138}{1000}$ as a decimal is 0·138.

Think together

1 What decimals are represented on each of these thousandth grids?

a)

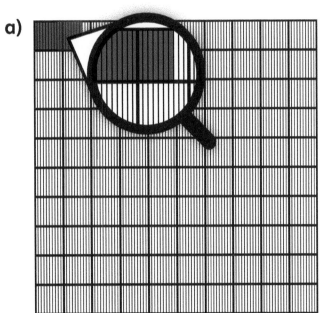

c)

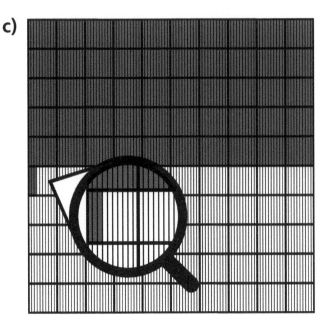

b)

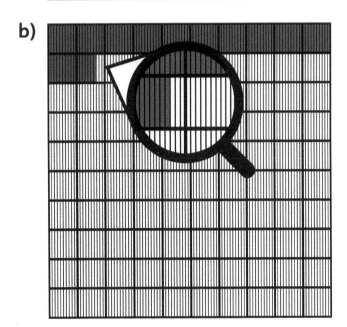

2 What decimal is shown here?

3 Amelia has these counters.

a) What decimal number has Amelia made?

b) Write Amelia's number as a fraction.

I know that 0·01 is equal to 1 hundredth.

I wonder how many hundredths 0·1 is equal to.

111

→ **Practice book 5B p80**

Thousandths on a place value grid

Discover

Danny

Emma

1 a) Represent the mass of the toy train on a place value grid.

b) What is the value of each of the digits in the number 0·852?

Share

a) 0·852 is made up of 8 tenths.

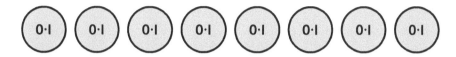

0·852 is made up of 5 hundredths.

0·852 is made up of 2 thousandths.

> I put these counters in a place value grid.

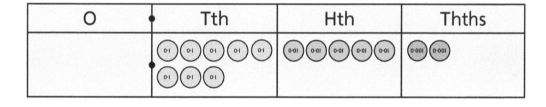

b) The columns help you work out the value of each digit.

The 8 is equal to 0·8 or 8 tenths.

The 5 is equal to 0·05 or 5 hundredths.

The 2 is equal to 0·002 or 2 thousandths.

Think together

1 What numbers are represented here?

a)

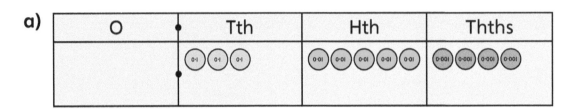

O		Tth	Hth	Thths
		⓪·ⓘ ⓪·ⓘ ⓪·ⓘ	⓪·ⓞⓘ ⓪·ⓞⓘ ⓪·ⓞⓘ ⓪·ⓞⓘ ⓪·ⓞⓘ	⓪·ⓞⓞⓘ ⓪·ⓞⓞⓘ ⓪·ⓞⓞⓘ ⓪·ⓞⓞⓘ

b)

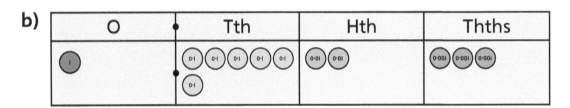

O		Tth	Hth	Thths
①		⓪·ⓘ ⓪·ⓘ ⓪·ⓘ ⓪·ⓘ ⓪·ⓘ	⓪·ⓞⓘ ⓪·ⓞⓘ	⓪·ⓞⓞⓘ ⓪·ⓞⓞⓘ ⓪·ⓞⓞⓘ
		⓪·ⓘ		

c)

0·1 0·1 0·1 0·1

0·001 0·001 0·001 0·001 0·001 0·001 0·001

2 What is the value of each of the underlined digits?

a)

| 0·6<u>3</u>7 | 12·18<u>9</u> |

b) Write down 3 numbers that have 7 hundredths in.

What do you notice about the numbers?

3 Alex has these digit cards and a decimal point card.

| 1 | 3 | 5 | 6 | 8 |

She chooses four digit cards to make a decimal number.

| 1 | . | 3 | 8 | 6 |

a) Represent Alex's number on a place value grid.

T	O	● Tth	Hth	Thths

b) What is the value of each of the digits?

c) How many different numbers less than 2 can Alex make?

> I think the columns help me work out the values of the digits.

→ Practice book 5B p83

Compare and order decimals – same number of decimal places

Discover

1 a) Order the results from smallest to largest. Who had the quickest reaction time?

   b) Convert the decimals to fractions. Use this to check the comparison made in a).

Share

a) The reaction times to compare have digits in the 1s and tenths columns.

5·9 has the fewest 1s, so this is the smallest.

6·2 and 6·5 have the same number of 1s, so we look at the tenths.

6·2 has the fewest tenths, so this is the next smallest number.

O		Tth
5	•	9
6	•	2
6	•	5

5·9 cm < 6·2 cm < 6·5 cm

The shorter the distance the quicker reaction time.

I used a number line to help me compare.

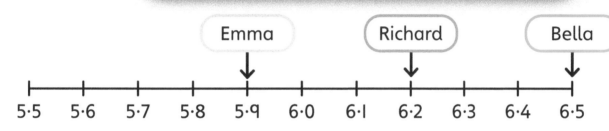

Emma's result was the shortest distance, so she had the quickest reaction time.

b)

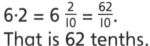

$6·2 = 6\frac{2}{10} = \frac{62}{10}$.
That is **62 tenths.**

$6·5 = 6\frac{5}{10} = \frac{65}{10}$.
That is **65 tenths.**

$5·9 = 5\frac{9}{10} = \frac{59}{10}$.
That is **59 tenths.**

59 tenths is less than 62 tenths which is less than 65 tenths.
59 < 62 < 65

Think together

  a) What decimal is represented on each grid?

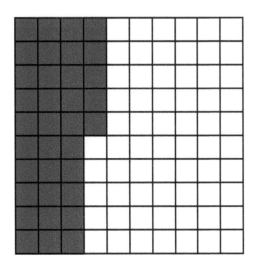   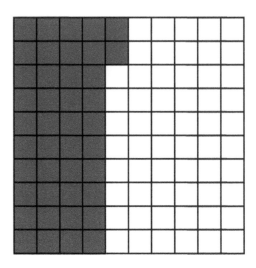

b) Which decimal is the greater?

2 **a)** Here are some more reaction time results.

Olivia	Andy	Mo
5·1 cm	4·1 cm	5·5 cm

Order the results from smallest to greatest.

☐ < ☐ < ☐

b) Here are the heights of the same children. Which child is the tallest?

Olivia — 1·45 m   Andy — 1·21 m   Mo — 1·49 m

3 Ambika and Kate are comparing decimals.

Ambika

Kate

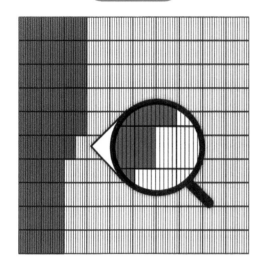

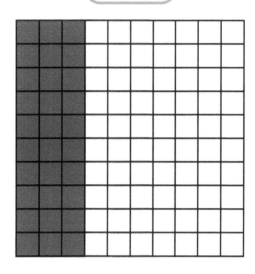

a) What decimals have they each made?

b) Which decimal is greater – Ambika's or Kate's?

I wonder if it helps to write them all as fractions.

I wrote each number to three decimal places, and then used a place value grid to compare them.

119

→ Practice book 5B p86

Compare and order any decimals with up to 3 decimal places

Discover

Name	Distance jumped (m)
Luis	3·42
Olivia	4·4
Isla	4·21

Luis

Olivia

You jumped 4·21 m, Isla!

Andy

Isla

1 **a)** Who is in first place, second place and third place?

b) Andy jumps and is now in second place.

How far could he have jumped?

120

Share

a) Luis jumps less than 4 m. Luis is in third place.

Start by comparing the column with the largest place value.

Name	O	•	Tth	Hth
Luis	① ① ①	•	0·1 0·1 0·1 0·1	0·01 0·01
Isla	① ① ① ①	•	0·1 0·1	0·01
Olivia	① ① ① ①	•	0·1 0·1 0·1 0·1	

4·4 m and 4·21 m have a different number of digits.

I used counters on a place value grid to help me.

First compare the ones, then the tenths, then the hundredths.

Both numbers have 4 ones, but 4·4 has more tenths than 4·21.

3·42 < 4·21 < 4·4

Luis is in third place, Isla is in second place, Olivia is in first place.

b) A decimal number line helps to show the possible distances that Andy could have jumped.

3rd place ↓

2nd place ↓   1st place ↓

3·4   3·5   3·6   3·7   3·8   4   4·1   4·2   4·3   4·4   4·5

Andy's jump could be any distance between 4·21 m and 4·4 m.

Think together

1 Here are the results from a 200 m sprint.

Use a place value grid to order the times from slowest to fastest.

Runner	Time
A	21·09 s
B	21·30 s
C	21·07 s
D	21·49 s
E	21·04 s

T	O	Tth	Hth

Slowest to fastest runners: ☐ > ☐ > ☐ > ☐ > ☐

2 A competition shot put is supposed to weigh **7·26 kg.**

4 shot put balls have been weighed. Which ones are too heavy, which are too light and which are the correct weight?

A

7·258 kg

B

7·3 kg

C

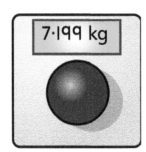

7·199 kg

D

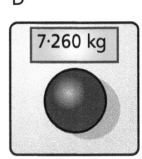

7·260 kg

3 Write a number that fits each description.

I will use a place value grid with counters to check my ideas.

I will convert the decimals into fractions to help.

a) A number between 4 and 4·1.

4   4·1

b) A number between 4·59 and 4·6.

4·59   4·6

c) A fraction that is greater than 0·6 and less than 0·61.

123

Round to the nearest whole number

Discover

1 **a)** Round the mass of each box to the nearest whole number.

b) A fifth box rounds to 9 kg. What could its mass be?

Share

a) Each of the four boxes has a mass of between 9 kg and 10 kg.

To round to the nearest whole number, work out if it is nearer to 9 or nearer to 10.

> I drew a number line and marked it in tenths. Now I can see that 9·2 and 9·3 are nearer to 9, and 9·8 is nearer to 10.

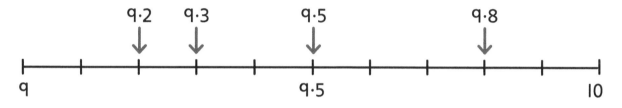

> 9·5 is exactly half-way between 9 and 10. The half-way number always rounds up.

9·2 and 9·3 round to 9 kg to the nearest whole number.

9·5 and 9·8 round to 10 kg to the nearest whole number.

b) 8·5 rounds to 9, but 9·5 rounds to 10. The mass of the box is between 8·5 kg and 9·49 kg.

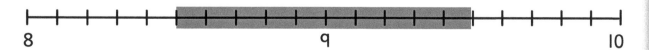

Think together

1 Four numbers are marked on a number line.

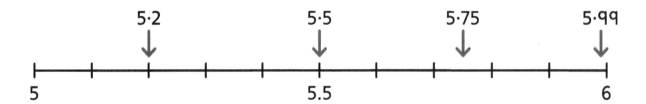

Round each number to the nearest whole number.

2 Round each number in these two sets to the nearest whole number.

Set A

2·4   3·4   8·4   II·4   38·4

Set B

3·65   3·61   3·62   3·69   3·648

3 **a)** Ebo is trying to round a number to the nearest whole number.

The number is marked by the arrow on the number line.

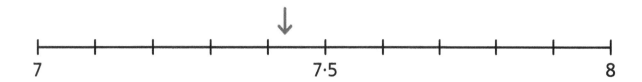

7   7·5   8

I'm not sure I can round my number to the nearest whole number if I don't know what it is.

Ebo

Is Ebo correct?

b) A number rounds to 6 to the nearest whole number.

Write down 5 numbers it could be.

What is the smallest number it could be?

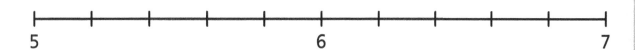

5   6   7

→ Practice book 5B p92

Round to one decimal place

Discover

1 **a)** Where would 2·36 appear on the number line?

b) Round 2·36 to the nearest tenth.

Share

a) The number line goes up in hundredths.

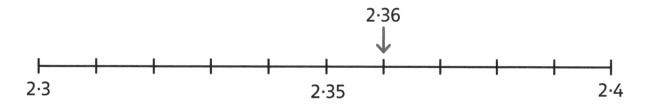

b) 2·3 and 2·4 are the previous and next tenths.

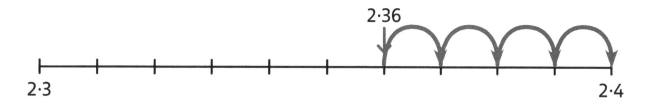

There are 4 hundredths between 2·36 and 2·4.

There are 6 hundredths between 2·36 and 2·3.

2·36 is closer to 2·4 than 2·3.

I saw from the number line that 2·36 is closer to 2·4 than 2·3.

2·36 rounds to 2·4 to the nearest tenth.

Rounding to the nearest tenth is also called rounding to 1 decimal place.

Think together

1 **a)** Round each of these numbers to the nearest tenth.

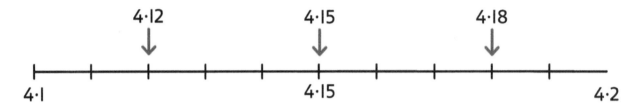

b) Round each number to one decimal place

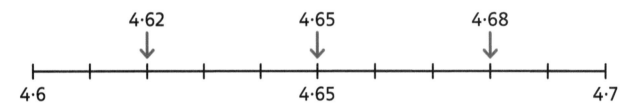

2 Round each of these numbers to one decimal place.

| 1·67 | 1·672 | 23·67 | 2·367 | 9·345 |

I understand it more deeply when I draw a number line.

I can tell which numbers will round up or down by looking at the hundredths digit.

130

3 **a)** Round 1·24 to the nearest whole number.

1   2

b) Round 1·24 to the nearest tenth.

1·2   1·3

c) A number rounds to 1·2 to the nearest tenth.

What could the number have been?

1·2

I will also try using a place value grid to help with the rounding.

131

→ Practice book 5B p95

Understand percentages

Discover

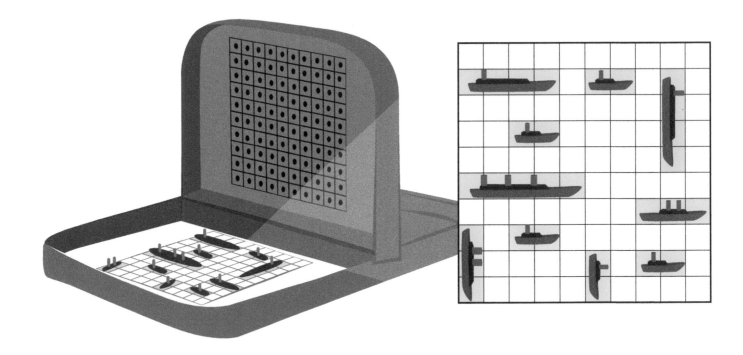

1 **a)** Alex has placed her ships on the grid.

How much of the grid is covered?

How much of the grid is empty?

b) She removes the two ships below.

Now how much of the grid is covered and how much is empty?

Share

> I moved the ships side by side to make it easier to work out.

a) The grid is 10 rows of 10 squares.

$10 \times 10 = 100$

There are 100 squares in total.

The ships cover 29 out of 100 squares.

$100 - 29 = 71$

So 71 squares out of 100 are not covered.

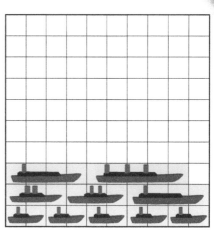

> Per cent (%) means 'parts out of 100'. So 1 per cent means 1 part out of 100 or $\frac{1}{100}$. 10 per cent means 10 parts out of 100 or $\frac{10}{100}$.

Percentages can describe this situation.

29% of the grid is covered.

71% of the grid is empty.

b) The two ships covered $4 + 3 = 7$ squares.

$29 - 7 = 22$

So now only 22 out of 100 are covered.

22% of the grid is covered.

$100 - 22 = 78$

So now 78 out of 100 squares are uncovered.

78% of the grid is empty.

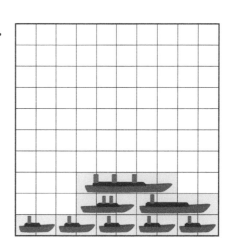

Think together

1) What percentage is shaded in these diagrams?

a)

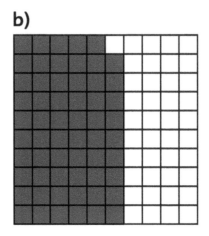

b)

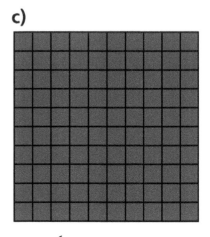

c)

In one of these hundredths grids the whole is shaded. I wonder if that is 1%.

2) Each of the pictures represents a percentage.

Which one is the odd one out?

A

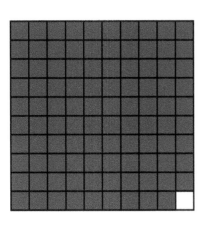

B

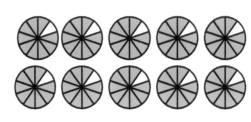

C

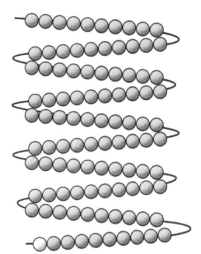

3 **a)** Emma and Zac are discussing 1% and 100%. Do you agree with Emma or Zac?

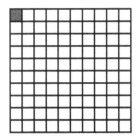
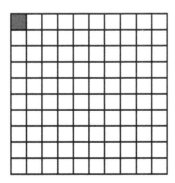
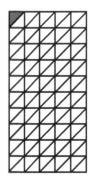

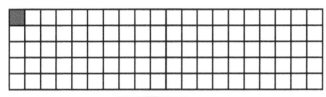

These all show different percentages, because they are different shapes and sizes.

Emma

No, I think these all show the same percentage. Each percentage looks different because each whole is a different shape or size.

Zac

b) Max has drawn a diagram. He says it shows 1%. Do you agree?

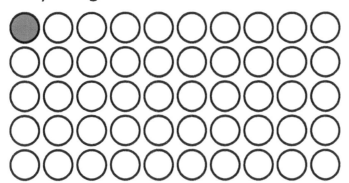

135

Percentages as fractions and decimals

Discover

Jamilla

1 **a)** Find two sets of three matching cards.

b) Write a fraction and draw a diagram to match the remaining card.

Share

I started with the diagram cards.

Each shows 100 equal parts. This represents hundredths.

a) Card D shows 28 squares shaded out of 100. This can be written as 28% (Card A) and as $\frac{28}{100}$ (Card G).

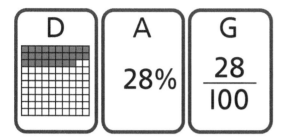

Card F shows 2 squares shaded out of 100. This can be written as 2% (Card E) and as $\frac{2}{100}$. $\frac{2}{100}$ is 2 hundredths which is equivalent to the decimal 0·02 (Card B).

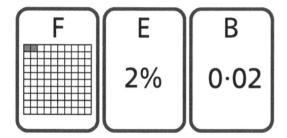

b) The remaining card is Card C, which shows 22%.

22% is 22 equal parts out of 100 and so can be written as $\frac{22}{100}$.

This can be represented on a hundredths grid like this:

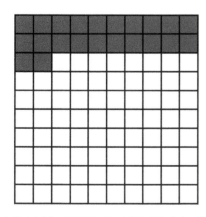

We can say 22% = $\frac{22}{100}$. The percentage and the fraction are equivalent.

Think together

1 Write the numbers represented by each diagram as a fraction, decimal and percentage.

a)

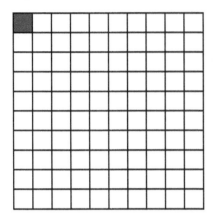

b)

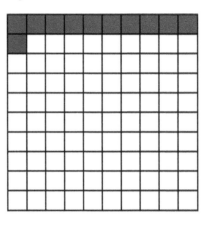

c)

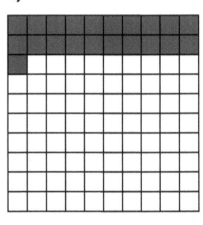

2 Put the fractions, decimals and percentages into the correct place in the table.

70% $\frac{12}{100}$ 5%   0·09 $\frac{5}{100}$ 0·7   9%   0·12

Fraction	Decimal	Percentage
$\frac{9}{100}$	☐	☐
☐	0·05	☐
☐	☐	12%
$\frac{70}{100}$	☐	☐

CHALLENGE

3   **a)**   Ambika and Richard are talking about saving their pocket money.

I have saved 100% of my pocket money.

I have saved 100% of mine. We must have saved the same!

Ambika

Richard

Explain why Richard could be wrong.

b)   Ambika wants to convert 100% into a decimal.

Show how to write 100% as a decimal.

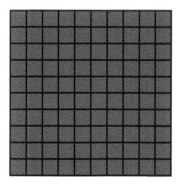

I think it could be 0·100.

I do not think that is right. 100% means 100 hundredths.

→ **Practice book 5B p101**

Equivalent fractions, decimals and percentages

Discover

Luis

1 a) Look at the pegboard in front of Luis. What fraction, percentage and decimal of the board is covered by circle pegs?

What fraction, percentage and decimal of the board is covered by square pegs?

b) What fraction, percentage and decimal of the board is covered by triangle pegs?

Share

a) The circle pegs fill 10 out of 100 spaces.   They fill 1 row out of 10.

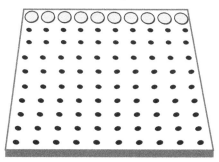

$\frac{1}{10} = 0\cdot1$

$\frac{10}{100} = 10\%$ $\frac{10}{100} = \frac{1}{10}$

$\frac{1}{10}$, 10% or 0·1 of the board is covered by circle pegs.

> I can say that $\frac{1}{10}$ is equivalent to 10% or 0·1.

The square pegs fill 30 out of 100 spaces. They fill 3 rows out of 10.

$\frac{3}{10}$ is equivalent to 30% or 0·3.

$\frac{3}{10}$, 30% or 0·3 of the board is covered by square pegs.

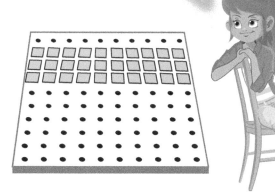

b) The triangle pegs are in 6 rows of 5.

$6 \times 5 = 30$

The triangle pegs fill 30 out of 100 spaces.

$\frac{30}{100} = \frac{3}{10} = 0\cdot3 = 30\%$

$\frac{3}{10}$, 30% or 0·3 of the board is covered by triangle pegs.

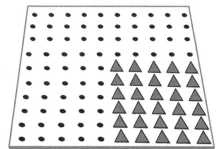

> It is still $\frac{3}{10}$, even though it is not 3 full rows.

Think together

1 Convert these decimals, fractions and percentages to complete the table.

Decimal	0·1	0·2	☐	☐	☐	1	0
Tenths	$\frac{1}{10}$	☐	☐	$\frac{8}{10}$	☐	☐	☐
Hundredths	$\frac{10}{100}$	☐	☐	☐	$\frac{90}{100}$	☐	☐
Percentage	10%	☐	40%	☐	☐	☐	☐

2 What fraction, decimal and percentage is shaded?

a)  b) 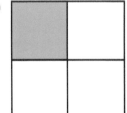 c)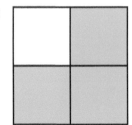

These diagrams are not split into 100 equal parts. I wonder how to find the percentages.

I will think about how I can describe the amount shaded.

CHALLENGE

3 **a)** Andy and Reena both took a test. Reena scored 30 out of 60. Andy scored 30%.

How can you compare their scores?

I will think about Reena's score as a fraction.

I can convert Reena's score to a percentage.

b) Emma has 40 marbles. 4 are blue.

What percentage are blue?

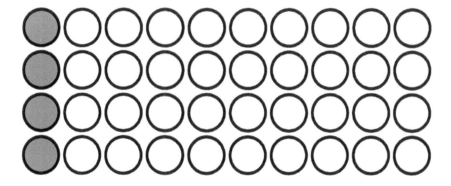

143

End of unit check

1 Which fraction is represented in the place value grid?

O		Tth
0		3

A $\frac{3}{10}$ B $\frac{10}{3}$ C $\frac{3}{100}$ D $\frac{1}{3}$

2 Which decimal is shown?

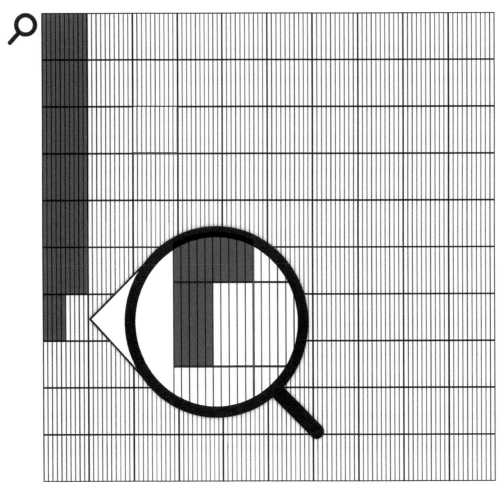

A 0·65 B 6·5 C 0·065 D 1·650

3 Which number would complete the statement correctly?

3·802 > ▢

A 3·9   B 3·81   C 3·8   D 4

4 What is 9·55 rounded to the nearest tenth?

A 9·5   B 9·65   C 10   D 9·6

5 Which pair is represented here?

A 0·9 and 9%

B $\frac{9}{100}$ and 90%

C 80% and $\frac{8}{10}$

D 90% and 0·9

6 Put these fractions, decimals and percentages in order from smallest to greatest.

0·3   13% $\frac{31}{100}$ 0·04 $\frac{2}{10}$ $\frac{131}{1,000}$

▢ ▢ ▢ ▢ ▢ ▢

Smallest ⟶ Greatest

→ Practice book 5B p107

Unit 10
Measure – perimeter and area

In this unit we will ...

⚡ Measure shapes to find their perimeter

⚡ Calculate the perimeter of polygons, squares, rectangles and other rectilinear shapes

⚡ Use a formula to find the area of squares and rectangles

How many rows? How many in each row? How many altogether?

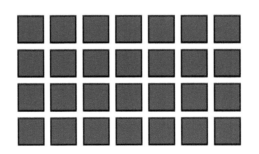

Here are some maths words we will be using. Which words are new?

perimeter · distance · area

length · width · polygon

centimetres (cm) · square centimetres (cm^2)

brackets · metres · square metres (m^2)

formula · compare · estimate · 2D shape

Which shape has the largest area? How do you know?

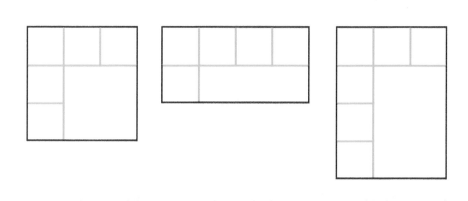

Perimeter of rectangles

Discover

1 a) What is the perimeter of the football pitch?

b) What is the length of the playground?

Share

a) Jamie and Ebo gave the length and the width of the football pitch.

I sketched a picture to help find the answer.

100 + 70 + 100 + 70 = 340 m

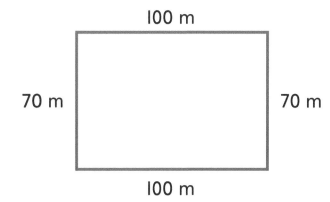

I added the length and width and then doubled the result.

100 + 70 = 170

170 × 2 = 340 m

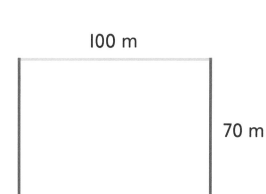

Brackets show which bit of the calculation to do first.

In this example, double the length and double the width before adding them together.

(70 × 2) + (100 × 2)

= 140 + 200

= 340 m

The perimeter of the football pitch is 340 metres.

b) The square playground has four sides all the same length.

50 m

perimeter = 200 m			
? m	? m	? m	? m

50 m   50 m

$200 \div 4 = 50$

50 m

The length of the playground is 50 metres because 50 m × 4 = 200 m.

Think together

1 A rugby pitch has a width of 70 metres and a length of 120 metres.

What is its perimeter?

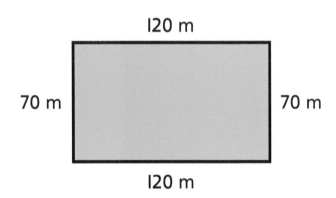

120 m

70 m   70 m

120 m

(length × 2) + (width × 2)

= (⬜ × 2) + (⬜ × 2)

= ⬜ + ⬜

= ⬜ m

I could use addition, but I can think of a quicker method using multiplication instead.

2 **a)** A square car park has a length of 40 metres.

What is its perimeter?

$\boxed{} \times \boxed{} = \boxed{}$

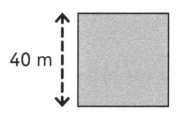

40 m

b) A square lawn has a perimeter of 80 metres.

What is its length?

$\boxed{} \div \boxed{} = \boxed{}$

80 m

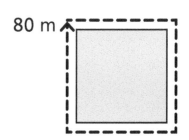

3 The length of a square is 25 cm.

Two squares are put together to make a rectangle.

CHALLENGE

I can't work out the perimeter of the rectangle because I don't know its length.

Amelia

The perimeter of the rectangle is double the perimeter of the square.

Danny

The perimeter of the rectangle is six times the length of the square.

Lee

Who is right? Explain your answer.

I am going to draw a quick sketch to help me work out what the rectangle looks like.

I am not sure if I need to count all the sides. I will check if any sides are inside the rectangle.

151

→ Practice book 5B p110

Perimeter of rectilinear shapes ❶

Discover

❶ **a)** What is the perimeter of the red stripy sticker?

b) Work out the perimeter of the blue dotty sticker without measuring all of the sides.

Share

a)

The perimeter of a 2D shape is the distance all around it.

There are no measurements labelled on the sticker, so I used a ruler to measure all the sides.

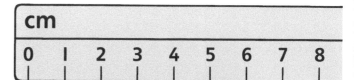

6 cm + 3 cm + 2 cm + 3 cm + 8 cm + 6 cm = 28 cm

The perimeter of the red stripy sticker is 28 cm.

b)

Rectangles have two pairs of equal sides, so I only needed to measure two of the sides. I added these, then doubled that result.

10 cm + 3 cm = 13 cm

13 × 2 = 26 cm

I doubled the length, doubled the width and added them.

10 cm × 2 = 20 cm

3 cm × 2 = 6 cm

20 + 6 = 26 cm

The perimeter of the blue dotty sticker is 26 cm.

Think together

1 What is the perimeter of this sticker?

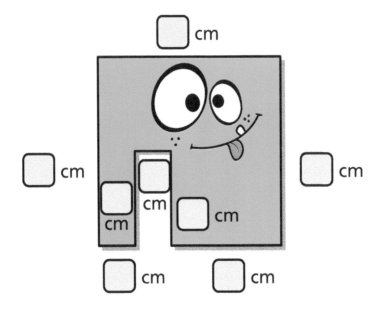

2 This sticker was a rectangle. What was its perimeter?

Explain how you know.

3 You have been asked to find the perimeter of this shape by only measuring two sides.

Point to the two sides you would choose to measure.

Explain how you can use them to find the answer.

I can see some sides that combine together.

Perimeter of rectilinear shapes ❷

Discover

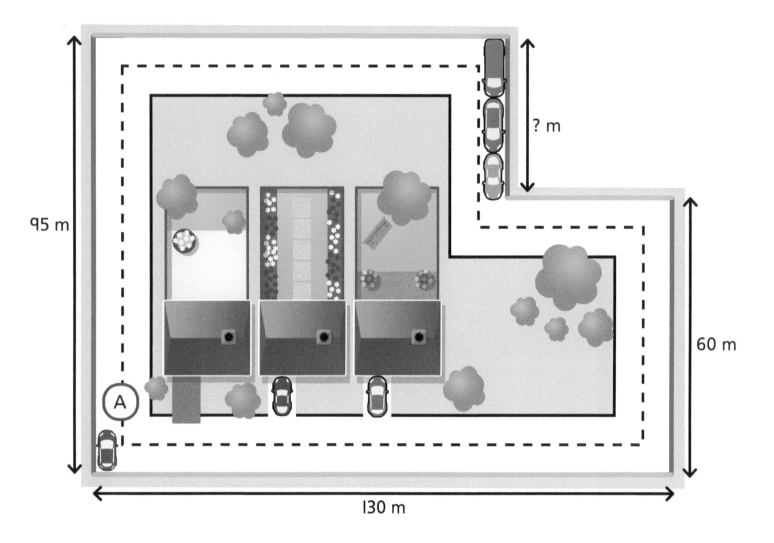

1 **a)** How long is the queue of three vehicles?

b) Car A drives all the way around the road once.

How far does it travel?

Share

a)

I used some of the side lengths I already knew to help find the missing length.

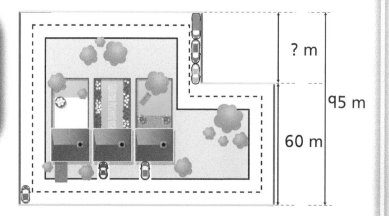

95 m – 60 m = 35 m

The length of the queue of three vehicles is 35 metres.

b) Work out the missing lengths then add to find the distance travelled.

130 + 35 + 60 + 130 + 95 = 450

The car travels 450 metres.

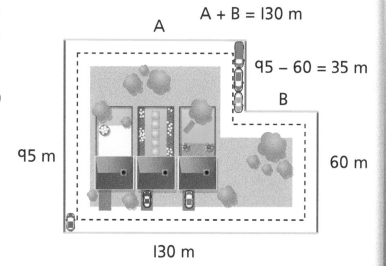

A + B = 130 m

95 – 60 = 35 m

The sides can combine to make double the length and double the width.

(130 × 2) + (95 × 2) = 260 + 190 = 450

Car A travels 450 metres.

I found the answer by using doubling!

Think together

1 This is a race track.

a) Complete these number sentences with the correct letters.

$\boxed{}$ + $\boxed{}$ = 250 m

$\boxed{}$ + $\boxed{}$ = 300 m

b) Find the perimeter of the track.

($\boxed{}$ × 2) + ($\boxed{}$ × 2)

= $\boxed{}$ + $\boxed{}$

= $\boxed{}$ m

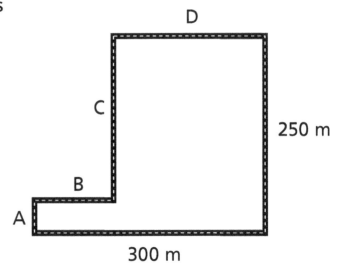

D

C

250 m

B

A

300 m

2 This diagram shows the shape of a playground.

What is the perimeter of the playground?

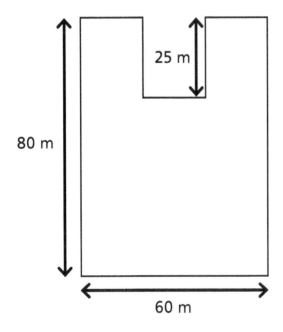

25 m

80 m

60 m

Even though only some of these sides are labelled, I think I can see what the others are equal to.

③ Lexi has two cardboard rectangles the same size.

42 cm

15 cm

She puts the rectangles together to make a new shape.

What is its perimeter?

42 cm

15 cm

I have spotted a way to work out the missing side length using what I know already.

I know all the side lengths except one.

159

Perimeter of polygons

Discover

1 **a)** Which shapes have sides of equal length?

b) Calculate the perimeter of each shape.

Share

a)

1 cm

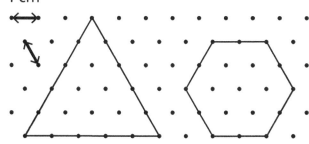 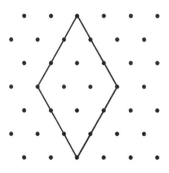

Each of these shapes is a regular polygon. The sides are of equal length, and all of the angles are equal.

This shape has 4 equal sides, but the angles are different.

b) Calculate the perimeters in one step.

1 cm

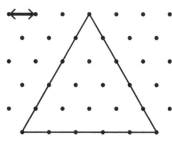 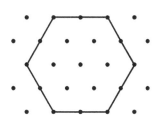 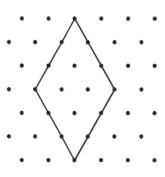

3 × 5 = 15

The perimeter is 15 cm.

6 × 2 = 12

The perimeter is 12 cm.

4 × 3 = 12

The perimeter is 12 cm.

Calculate the perimeter in two steps.

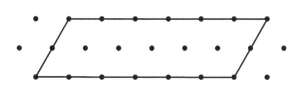

2 × 7 = 14   2 × 2 = 4

14 + 4 = 18

The perimeter is 18 cm.

Think together

I will use efficient calculations.

① Calculate the perimeter of each polygon.

a)

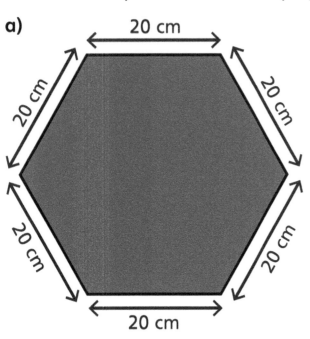

b)

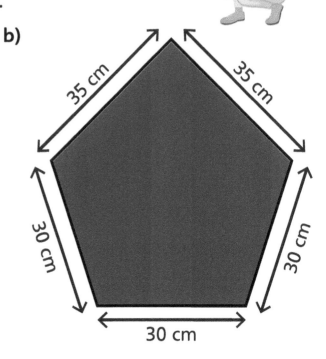

② Each polygon has a perimeter of 300 mm. Calculate the length of the sides. In each polygon, every side is equal in length.

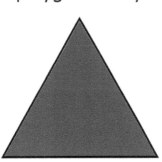

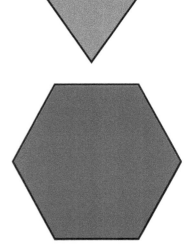

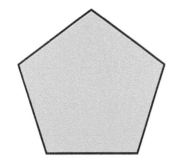

3 Use dotted paper like this to answer this question.

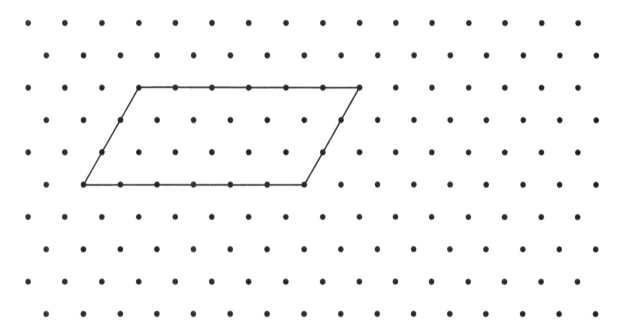

a) Draw a different quadrilateral with the same perimeter as this parallelogram.

b) Draw a pentagon with the same perimeter as this parallelogram.

c) Draw a hexagon with the same perimeter as this parallelogram.

I will use my own dotted paper and count the dots carefully.

→ Practice book 5B p119

Area of rectangles ❶

Discover

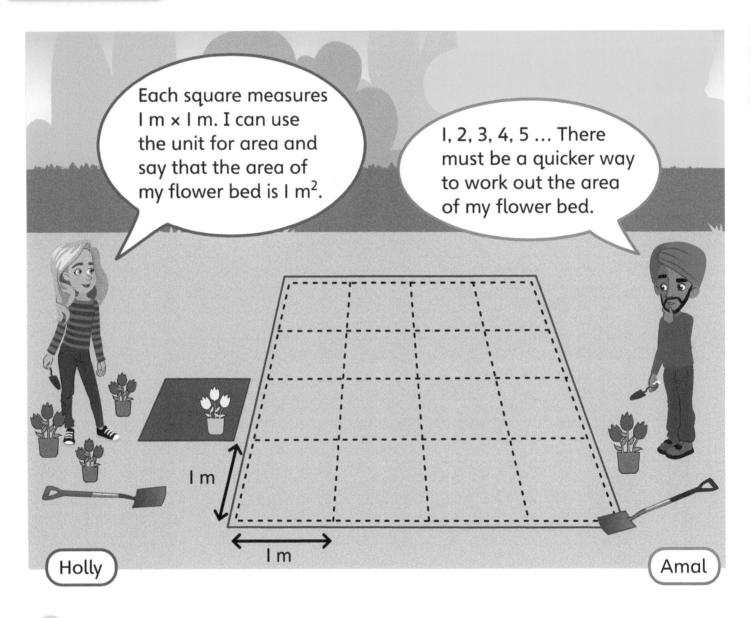

❶ a) What will the area of Amal's flower bed be?

b) A third gardener digs a rectangular flower bed with an area of 8 m².

What could its length and width be?

Share

a)

I found the area by counting each of the squares separately.

The metre squares make a 4 × 4 array. I used this fact to find the area more quickly!

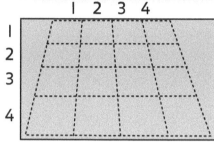

There are 4 rows of squares.

Each row contains 4 squares.

$4 \times 4 = 16$

There are 16 metre squares altogether.

The area of Amal's flower bed will be 16 m².

b) Number of rows × number of columns = total number of squares

$$\text{length} \quad \times \quad \text{width} \quad = \quad \text{area}$$

I knew the length and the width must be two numbers that multiply together to make 8.

Formula for area of a rectangle:
$a = l \times w$

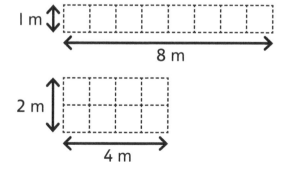

$1 \text{ m} \times 8 \text{ m} = 8 \text{ m}^2$

$2 \text{ m} \times 4 \text{ m} = 8 \text{ m}^2$

The length and width could either be 8 m × 1 m or 4 m × 2 m.

Think together

1   What is the area of this flower bed?

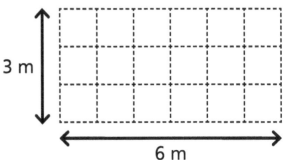

There are ☐ rows of metre squares.

Each row contains ☐ squares.

☐ × ☐ = ☐

There are ☐ metre squares altogether.

The area of the flower bed is ☐ m^2.

2   What is the area of these rectangles?

a)

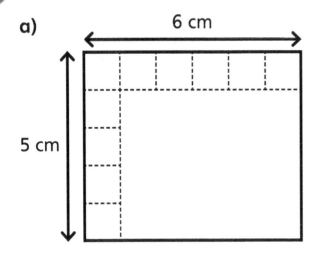

b)

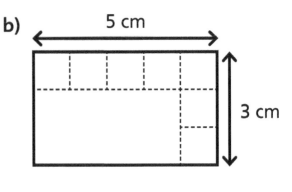

3 How many different rectangles can you make that have an area of 24 cm²? Explain how you know.

I am going to use a table to record my results.

I can think of a way to order them so we do not miss any out!

→ Practice book 5B p122

Area of rectangles ❷

Discover

① **a)** Which window has the larger area, A or B?

b) What is the area of window C in square metres (m²)?

Share

a) Each small pane of glass has an area of 1 square metre.

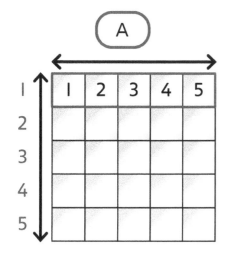

A has 5 rows of 5 panes.

5 × 5 = 25 panes

The area of window A is 25 m².

B has 3 rows of 8 panes.

3 × 8 = 24 panes

The area of window B is 24 m².

25 > 24, so window A has the larger area.

b)

I used length × width to work out the area of window C.

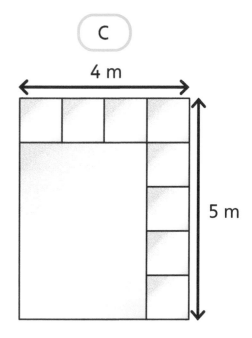

Area = length × width

Area of window C = 5 m × 4 m = 20 m.

The area of window C is 20 m².

Think together

1 Which shape has the larger area?

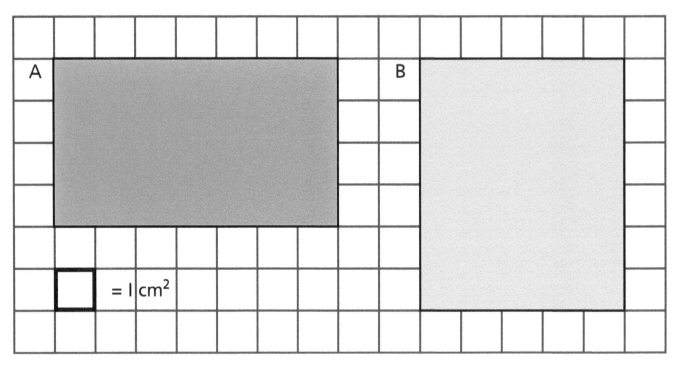

= 1 cm²

2 a) Use multiplication to find the area of these rectangles.

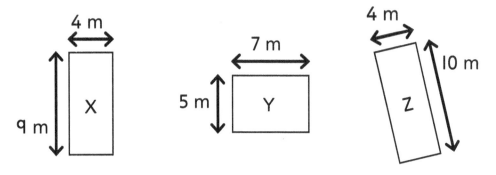

b) Order the rectangles from the largest to smallest area.

3 Kate and Aki have each drawn a rectangle.

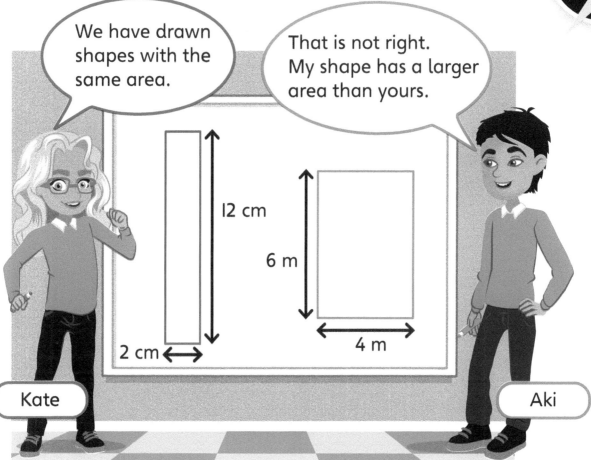

Kate: "We have drawn shapes with the same area."

Aki: "That is not right. My shape has a larger area than yours."

12 cm

6 m

2 cm

4 m

Kate

Aki

Who is correct?

Explain your answer.

"I will compare 2 × 12 with 4 × 6."

"I will look at the units of measure too. That will help me answer the question."

171

Area of compound shapes

Discover

1 **a)** The class have made rectangles from tissue paper.

What is the area of rectangle A?

What is the area of rectangle B?

b) What is the area of the compound shape C?

Share

a) Area = length × width.

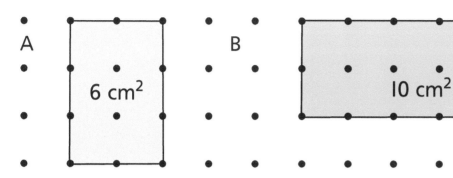

$3 \times 2 = 6$

The area is 6 cm².

$2 \times 5 = 10$

The area is 10 cm².

This is a **compound shape** made by joining shape A and shape B along an edge.

b)

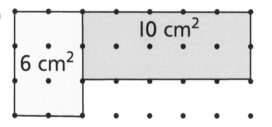

$6 + 10 = 16$

The area is 16 cm².

I wonder if you can always just add the areas of rectangles to find the area of a compound shape.

I made my own compound shapes to explore further.

Think together

1   Calculate the area of each rectangle. Use your answers to calculate the area of each compound shape.

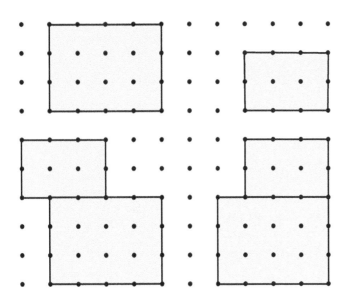

2   Calculate the area of each compound shape.

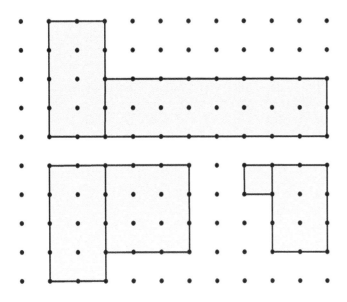

I will split them into rectangles.

3 Calculate the area of these compound shapes.

a)

5 m

10 m

15 m

30 m

I will work out the missing lengths first.

b)

60 m

20 m

40 m

50 m

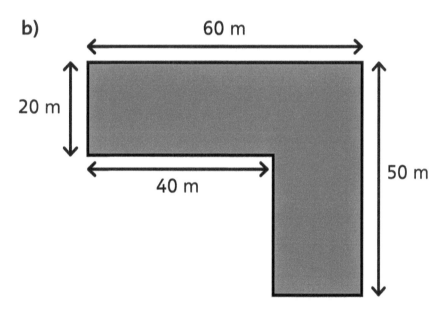

I can see different ways to split each shape into rectangles.

→ Practice book 5B p128

Estimate area

Discover

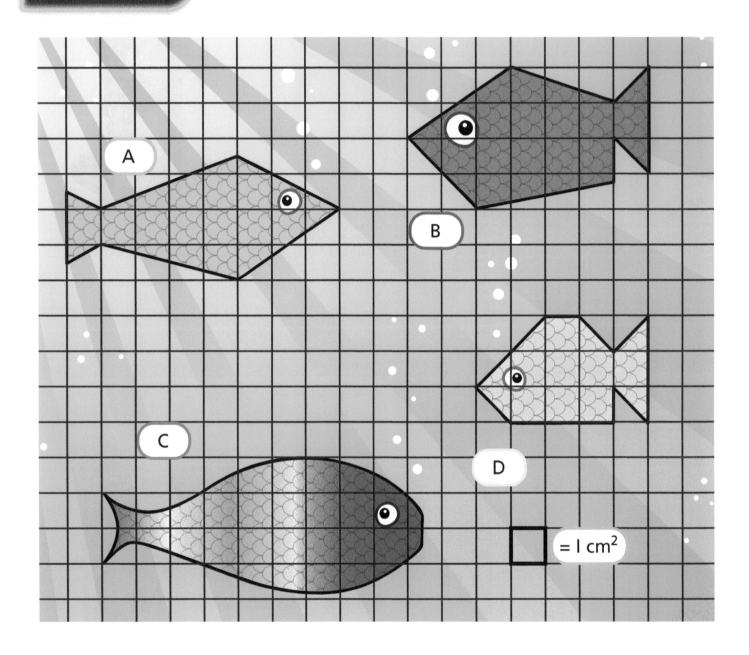

1 **a)** How can you estimate the area of fish A?

b) Which fish has the largest area?

Share

a) When a shape is made of some whole squares and some part squares, you can estimate its area.

We started by counting the whole squares.

Then we thought about the almost-whole squares, the half squares and those that are less than half.

There are 8 whole squares.

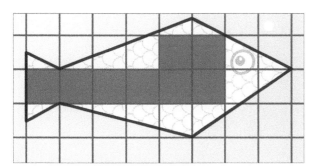

There are 6 almost-whole squares.

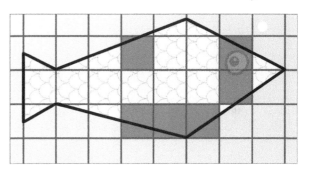

There is 1 half square.

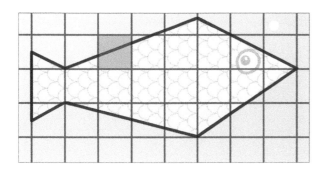

Ignore any squares that are less than half.

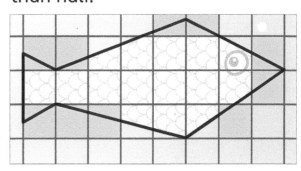

$8 + 6 + \frac{1}{2} + 0 = 14\frac{1}{2}$ squares

177

b) B 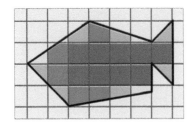 C 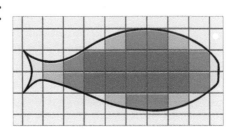 D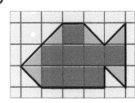

Fish	Whole squares	Almost-whole squares	Half squares	Estimated area (cm²)
A	8	6	1	$14\frac{1}{2}$
B	9	5	7 (= $3\frac{1}{2}$ whole squares)	$17\frac{1}{2}$
C	10	8	6 (= 3 whole squares)	21
D	8	0	6 (= 3 whole squares)	11

Fish C has the largest area.

Think together

1 Estimate the area of this crab.

☐ whole squares

☐ almost-whole squares

☐ half squares = ☐ squares

☐ + ☐ + ☐ = ☐ cm²

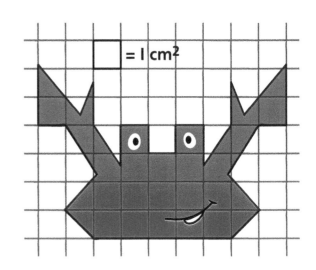

= 1 cm²

2 Use a table to estimate the area of the sails on this boat.

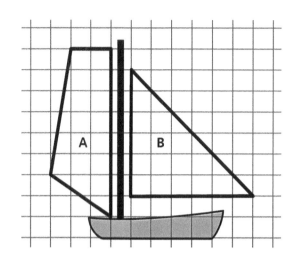

Sail	Whole squares	Almost-whole squares	Half squares	Less-than-half squares	Estimated area (squares)
A					
B					

3 Explain whether you think Flo or Astrid is correct.

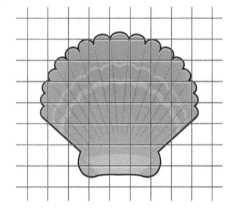

I think we should ignore them!

I want to count the squares that are less than half. They are part of the area too.

179

End of unit check

1 Use a ruler to measure the perimeter of this shape. What is it?

A 5 cm	**B** 15 cm	**C** 8 cm	**D** 16 cm

2 Which of these is **not** true?

A To find the perimeter of a rectangle, double the length and add it to double the width.

B To find the perimeter of a square, measure one side length and multiply it by 4.

C To find the perimeter of a rectangle, multiply the length by the width.

D To find the perimeter of a rectangle, measure each of the four sides and add them all together.

3 What is the perimeter of this field?

A 184 m

B 92 m

C 45 m

D 47 m

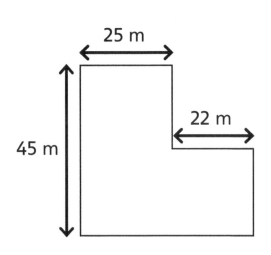

4 A square has a side length of 7 cm. What is its area?

A 28 cm²   B 49 cm²   C 7 cm²   D 49 cm

5 An equilateral triangle has a perimeter of 21 cm. What is the length of one side?

A 63 cm   B 7 cm   C 6 cm   D 3 cm

6 What is the side marked A?

A 3 m

B 5 m

C 7 m

D 10 m

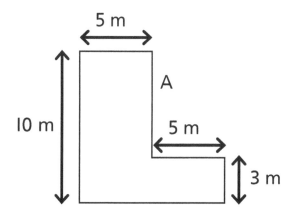

7 A gardener has planted a square flower bed in the middle of a square lawn.

The flower bed has an area of 36 m².

The lawn is the shaded area on the diagram.

What is the area of the lawn?

⬚ m²

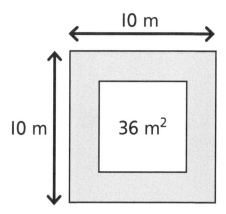

→ **Practice book 5B p134**

Unit 11
Graphs and tables

In this unit we will ...

⚡ Draw simple line graphs

⚡ Read information from tables

⚡ Understand and create two-way tables

⚡ Read information from line graphs

⚡ Answer questions relating to the information in graphs and tables

⚡ Read and understand simple timetables

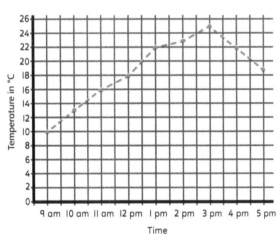

You will be able to draw a line graph from data in a table. Can you see how this line graph has been drawn?

Time	9 am	10 am	11 am	12 pm	1 pm	2 pm	3 pm	4 pm	5 pm
Temp (°C)	10	13	16	18	22	23	25	22	19

We will need some maths words. How many of these can you remember?

graph   line graph   table

dual line graph   horizontal   vertical

two-way table   scale   axis/axes   vertical axis

horizontal axis   data   kilometres (km)   kilograms (kg)

plot/plotted   tallies/tally   timetable

You can think of the axes like number lines. What numbers are missing from this number line? What are the arrows pointing to?

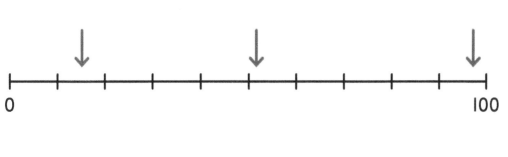

0   100

Draw line graphs

Discover

Day	Mon	Tues	Wed	Thurs	Fri	Sat	Sun
Number of cars sold	8	5	7	12	15	19	17

Please could you draw a line graph of our car sales from last week.

1 **a)** The sales people have been asked to draw a line graph.

What should they think about before they start?

b) Draw a line graph to show the car sales data.

Share

a)

I think the days should go on the **horizontal axis** and sales on the **vertical axis**.

Amal

We need to work out a scale for the sales. I think we should go from 0 to 20 in 2s. Otherwise the **graph** might be too big.

Holly

Before drawing the graph, the sales people need to think about:

- what to show on each of the **axes**
- the scale on each of the axes.

b)

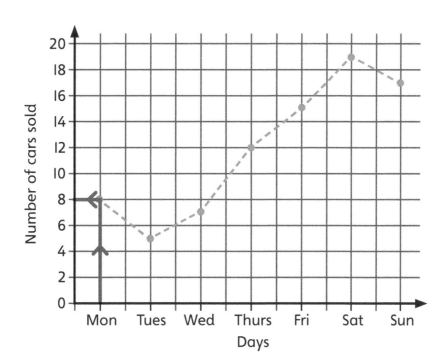

I drew and labelled the two axes first.

I **plotted** each point. For Monday, I plotted my point at 8 because 8 cars were sold on Monday.

Think together

1   Mr Jones sells ice creams.

Day	Ice creams sold
Monday	7
Tuesday	15
Wednesday	22
Thursday	29
Friday	37

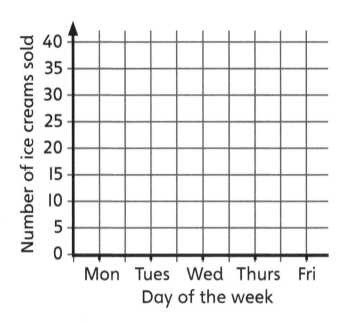

The table shows the number of ice creams he sold last week.

Plot this information on a line graph using squared paper.

2   Mr Jones also measured the temperature each day last week.

The line graph shows the temperature Mr Jones measured each day.

a) The temperature on Monday was ⁻3 °C.

    The temperature on Friday was 11 °C.

    Complete this graph using squared paper.

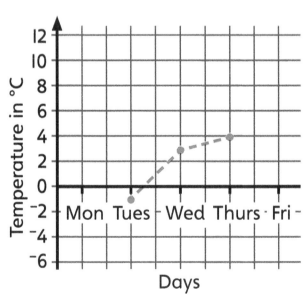

b) Use the information on the line graphs in Question 1 and Question 2 to compare the temperatures with the ice cream sales. What do you notice?

3 Danny collected some information about the population of his village and recorded it in this table.

He then drew this line graph using the information from the table.

Year	2017	2018	2019	2020	2021	2022	2023
Population	750	809	625	500	510	395	450

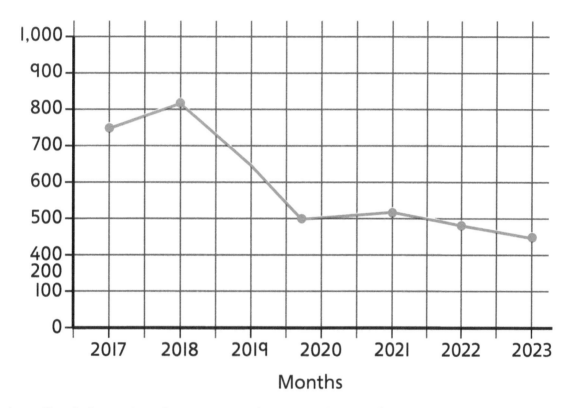

List all of the mistakes Danny has made in plotting and labelling his graph.

I will check whether the graph and the table show the same data.

I wonder if it is more useful to present this information in a graph or a table.

187

Read and interpret line graphs ①

Discover

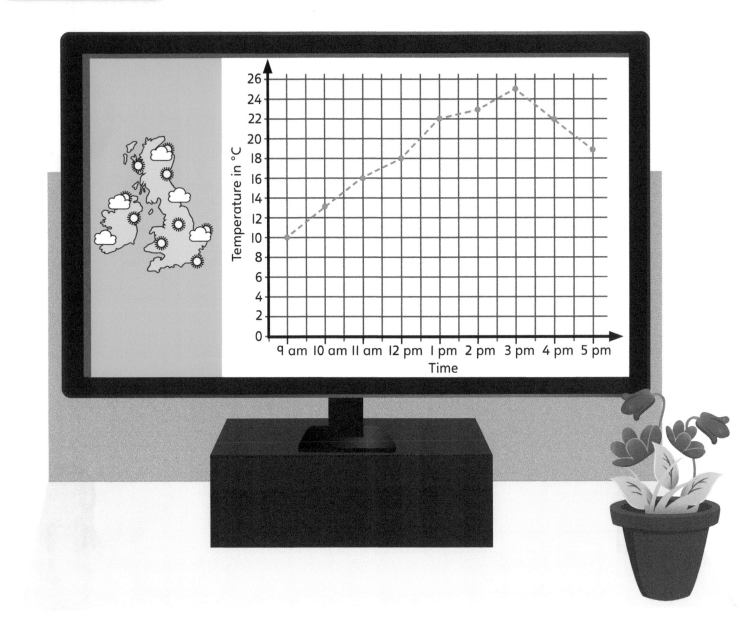

① **a)** What was the temperature at 11 am?

What was the temperature at 2 pm?

b) At which two times was the temperature 22 °C?

Share

a)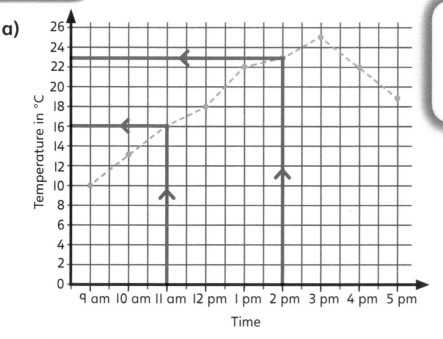

I drew vertical lines up and horizontal lines across to read the correct temperatures.

The temperature at 11 am was 16 °C.

The temperature at 2 pm was half-way between 22 °C and 24 °C, so it was 23 °C.

b)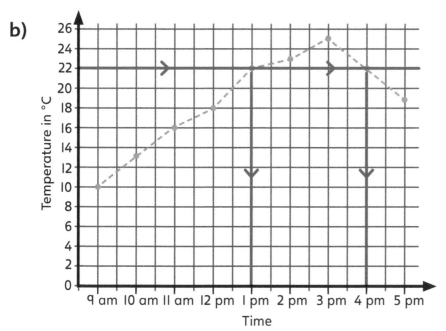

I started by finding 22 °C on the vertical axis.

The line graph shows that the temperature was 22 °C at 1 pm and at 4 pm.

189

Think together

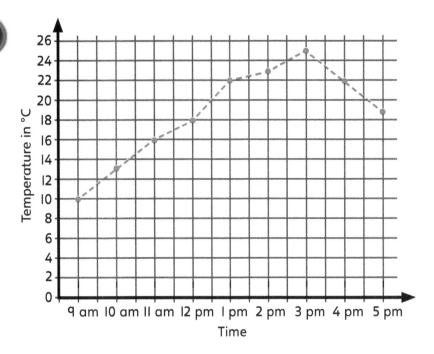

a) What was the highest recorded temperature during the day?

The highest recorded temperature during the day was ⬚ °C.

b) Estimate what the temperature was at 11:30 am.

The temperature at 11:30 am was about ⬚ °C.

2 Estimate how long the temperature was above 20 °C.

The temperature was above 20 °C for about ⬚ hours.

I think I can use the same method that I used to find the times when the temperature was 22 °C.

3 The line graph shows the number of children who were late during a week of school.

a) How many children were late on Thursday?

b) How many more children were late on Monday than on Tuesday?

c) Is Mr Jones's comment correct?

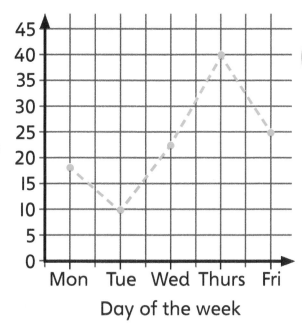

Number of children who were late

Day of the week

The graph shows that 100 different children were late this week.

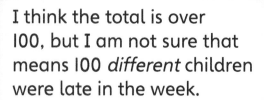

Mr Jones

I am going to work out the number of children late each day and record it in a table.

I think the total is over 100, but I am not sure that means 100 *different* children were late in the week.

191

Read and interpret line graphs ➋

Discover

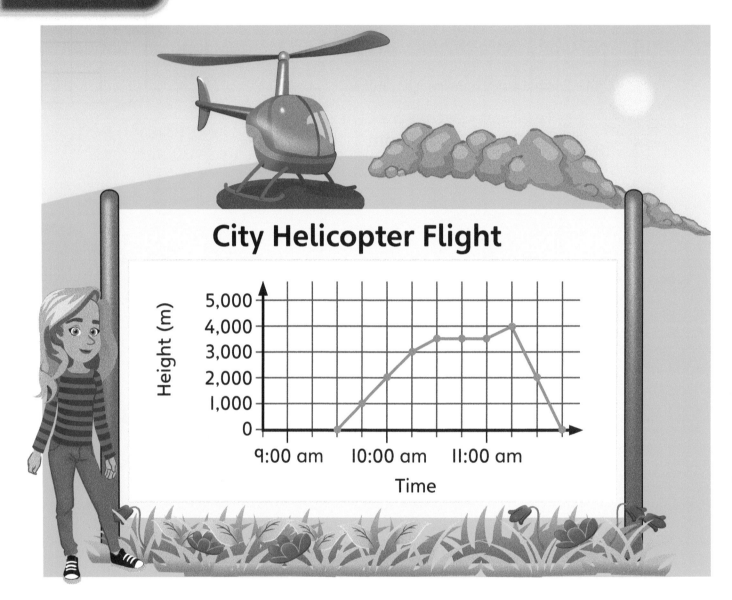

City Helicopter Flight

1   **a)** What is the height of the helicopter at 10:30 am?

How long does the helicopter stay at this height?

b) How long does the helicopter flight last?

Share

a)

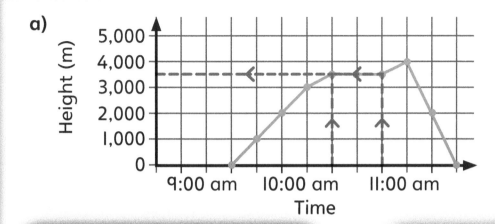

I drew a line up from 10:30 am and across to the height. The height is half-way between 3,000 and 4,000 metres.

I highlighted the graph where it shows the helicopter flying at 3,500 metres. This is a horizontal line.

The height of the helicopter at 10:30 am is 3,500 metres.

The helicopter stays at this height from 10:30 am to 11:00 am.

This is half an hour or 30 minutes.

b) The helicopter flight starts at 9:30 am. The flight finishes at 11:45 am.

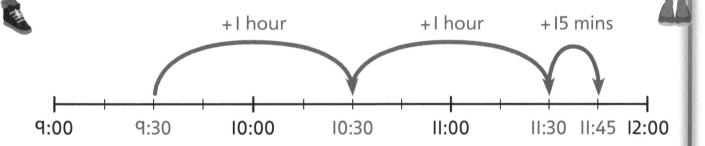

The helicopter flight lasts 2 hours and 15 minutes or $2\frac{1}{4}$ hours.

Think together

A **dual line graph** shows two sets of information on the same graph.

1 This dual line graph shows the average daily temperature in two cities.

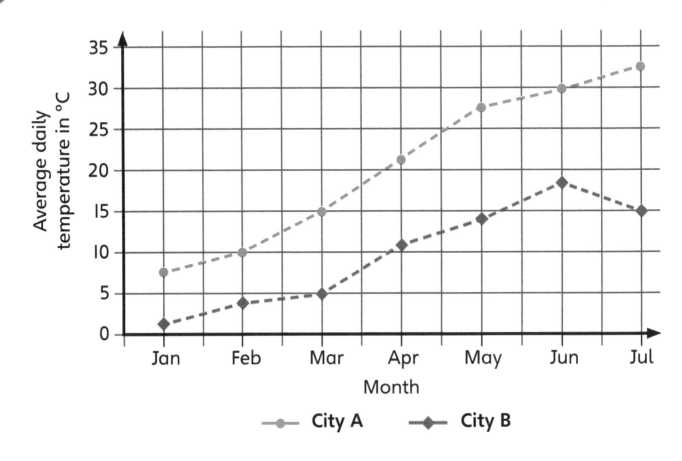

a) What is the temperature in City A in March? ☐ °C

b) What is the temperature in City B in June? ☐ °C

c) In April, how many degrees warmer is it in City A than in City B?

In April, City A is ☐ °C warmer than City B.

d) Which city is warmer?

City ☐ is warmer.

Explain to a partner how the graph shows this.

2 Toshi and Jen are flying a drone.

Here is a graph that shows the journey of the drone.

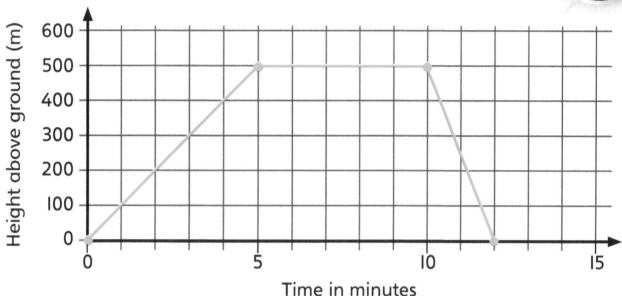

Which of the following statements are true? Explain your reasons.

- The drone starts from the ground.

- For the first 5 minutes, the drone's height increases by 100 metres every minute.

- When it reaches 500 metres the drone flies at this height for 7 minutes.

- The drone returns to the ground after 15 minutes in the air.

I will check the start and finish times and the heights after each minute to find the increase in height and to see how long the drone stays at the same height.

I think the drone stays at the same height when the line doesn't go up or down, but is horizontal.

195

Read and interpret tables

Discover

Last Week's Sales

Day	Number of loaves sold
Monday	127
Tuesday	195
Wednesday	88
Thursday	152
Friday	123

1 **a)** In total, how many loaves of bread were sold on Monday and Thursday?

b) The bakery makes 200 loaves every day.

How many loaves were **not** sold on Friday?

Share

a)

Day	Number of loaves sold
Monday	127
Tuesday	195
Wednesday	88
Thursday	152
Friday	123

?

127	152

I used column addition to work out the total.

	H	T	O
	1	2	7
+	1	5	2
	2	7	9

127 loaves of bread were sold on Monday.

152 loaves of bread were sold on Thursday.

In total, 279 loaves of bread were sold on Monday and Thursday.

b) 200 loaves of bread were made on Friday.

123 loaves of bread were sold on Friday.

	H	T	O
	¹2̸	⁹9̸0	¹0
–	1	2	3
	0	7	7

Method 1

200

123	?

Method 2

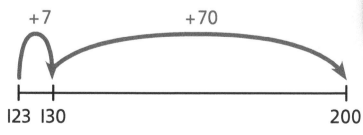

+7   +70

123 130   200

I used a number line to work out what I needed to add on.

77 loaves were **not** sold on Friday.

197

Think together

1 The table shows the weight of five dogs.

Name	Arnie	Buddy	Charlie	Digga	Ernie
Weight (kg)	23	19	26	23	20

a) How much does Ernie weigh?

Ernie weighs ⬚ kg.

b) Which two dogs are the same weight?

Both _____ and _____ are the same weight.

c) How much more does Charlie weigh than Buddy?

Charlie weighs ⬚ kg. Buddy weighs ⬚ kg.

⬚ – ⬚ = ⬚

Charlie weighs ⬚ kg more than Buddy.

d) The vet says a dog is overweight if it weighs more than 24 kg. Are any of the dogs overweight? If so, which ones?

e) Another dog, Rufus, has a weight that is in between Buddy's and Ernie's weight. How much could Rufus weigh?

Rufus could weigh ⬚ kg.

2 The table shows how many kilometres (km) Alex walks each day.

Day	Mon	Tue	Wed	Thur	Fri
Distance (km)	5	6	3·5	7·5	

Alex wants to walk 30 km in total.

How many more kilometres does she need to walk on Friday?

Alex needs to walk ☐ more kilometres on Friday.

3·5 is the same as $3\frac{1}{2}$.

3 Children were asked to choose their favourite colour.

CHALLENGE

Favourite colour	Number of children
Pink	12
Blue	10
Red	11
Green	4
Yellow	2
Other	1

I remember from my work earlier that to find $\frac{1}{4}$ I divide by 4.

The results were put into a table.

Holly says that more than $\frac{1}{4}$ of the children preferred blue.

Is Holly correct?

Explain how you know.

I will find the total number of children, then halve and halve again.

199

Two-way tables

Discover

1 **a)** Amal wants to sort out the socks from the hats and the spots from the stripes. Complete the two-way table to help him.

	Spots	Stripes
Socks		
Hats		

b) How many more socks than hats are there?

How did you find out your answer?

Share

a)

I used **tallies**. The first item is a sock that has stripes. I put this in the row that says socks and the column that says stripes.

	Spots	Stripes
Socks	~~||||~~ |||	||||
Hats	|||	~~||||~~

	Spots	Stripes
Socks	8	4
Hats	3	5

A two-way table shows two or more different sets of information.

b)

	Spots	Stripes	Total
Socks	8	4	12
Hats	3	5	8
Total	11	9	20

There are 12 socks and 8 hats.

12 − 8 = 4

There are 4 more socks than hats.

First, I worked out the total for each of the rows and each of the columns.

201

Think together

 The two-way table shows information about 50 people who went to the cinema last weekend.

	Saturday	Sunday	Total
Children	5	21	26
Adults	17	7	☐
Total	22	☐	50

Work out the missing totals then answer the following questions.

a) How many children went to the cinema on Saturday?

☐ children went to the cinema on Saturday.

b) In total, how many people went to the cinema on Sunday?

In total, ☐ people went to the cinema on Sunday.

c) On Sunday, how many more children than adults went to the cinema?

☐ more children than adults went to the cinema on Sunday.

d) On which day did the greatest number of people go to the cinema?

The greatest number of people went to the cinema

on _____ .

2 Two classes each have a fruit bowl.

The two-way table shows the fruit in each bowl.

Work with a partner to:

a) Complete the two-way table.

b) Write down five pieces of information the table shows you.

	Apples	Pears	Total
Class 5A	☐	18	30
Class 5B	14	☐	24
Total	26	28	☐

Use words such as total, difference, more and less.

3 The two-way table shows information on the number of ice creams sold.

CHALLENGE

a) Complete the two-way table.

b) What fraction of the ice creams sold were large cones?

		Cone size			
		Small	Medium	Large	Total
Flavour	Strawberry	2	12	42	☐
	Chocolate	☐	1	2	11
	Vanilla	☐	49	☐	☐
	Total	☐	☐	50	150

I know the total number of ice creams sold and how many large cones were sold.

203

→ Practice book 5B p148

Timetables

Discover

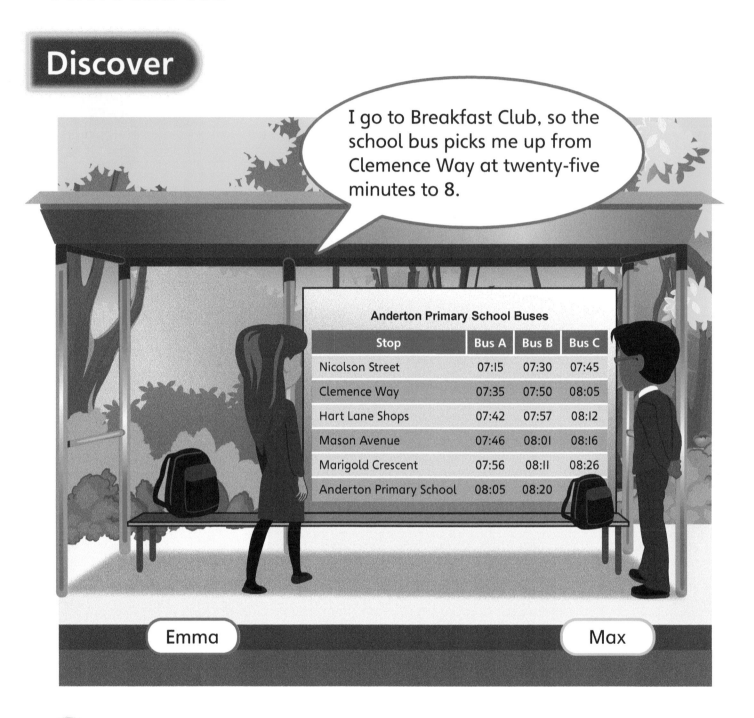

I go to Breakfast Club, so the school bus picks me up from Clemence Way at twenty-five minutes to 8.

Anderton Primary School Buses

Stop	Bus A	Bus B	Bus C
Nicolson Street	07:15	07:30	07:45
Clemence Way	07:35	07:50	08:05
Hart Lane Shops	07:42	07:57	08:12
Mason Avenue	07:46	08:01	08:16
Marigold Crescent	07:56	08:11	08:26
Anderton Primary School	08:05	08:20	

Emma

Max

1 **a)** What time does Emma arrive at school?

b) All the buses take the same amount of time to get to school. What time does Bus C arrive?

Share

A timetable shows the times when trains and buses depart and arrive. Timetables are usually written in 24-hour digital time, so you will have to convert first.

a) Each column of the timetable shows a different bus. Each row shows a different place.

Stop	Bus A
Nicolson Street	07:15
Clemence Way	07:35
Hart Lane Shops	07:42
Mason Avenue	07:46
Marigold Crescent	07:56
Anderton Primary School	08:05

→ Twenty-five minutes to 8
= 7:35 am
= 07:35

Emma catches Bus A.
Emma arrives at school at **08:05** (five minutes past 8).

b)

I used the information from the other buses to work out the hidden time.

Stop	Bus A	Bus C
Nicolson Street	07:15	07:45
Anderton Primary School	08:05	

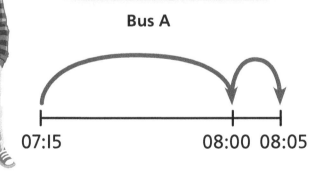

Bus A

07:15   08:00 08:05

Bus C

07:45   08:00   08:35

+ 15 minutes   + 35 minutes

+ 50 minutes

Each bus takes 50 minutes to get from Nicholson Street to school.

Bus C arrives at school at 08:35.

Think together

1 Look at this train timetable.

Littleborough	14:13	14:43	15:13	15:43
Birchfield	14:37	15:07	–	16:07
Ashtown Parkway	15:09	15:39	–	16:39
Ashtown Central	15:20	15:50	16:00	16:50

a) Isla gets on the 15:07 train at Birchfield.

What time does she arrive in Ashtown Central?

Isla arrives in Ashtown Central

at ☐ : ☐ .

Littleborough	14:43
Birchfield	15:07
Ashtown Parkway	15:39
Ashtown Central	15:50

b) Andy gets on the 14:13 train at Littleborough.

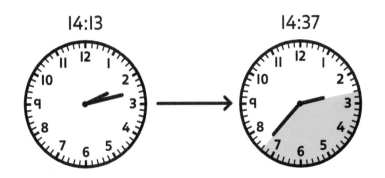

14:13   14:37

Littleborough	14:13
Birchfield	14:37
Ashtown Parkway	15:09
Ashtown Central	15:20

How long does it take to get to Birchfield?

It takes ☐ minutes to get to Birchfield.

2 How long does it take to get from Birchfield to Ashtown Parkway?

Littleborough	14:13
Birchfield	14:37
Ashtown Parkway	15:09
Ashtown Central	15:20

It takes ☐ minutes to get from Birchfield to Ashtown Parkway.

The journey crosses the o'clock boundary, so I am going to count in two jumps.

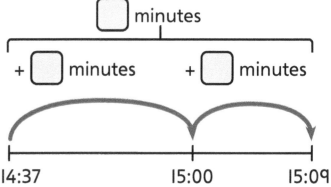

☐ minutes

+ ☐ minutes   + ☐ minutes

14:37   15:00   15:09

CHALLENGE

3 The 15:13 train from Littleborough to Ashtown Central is an express train. It does not stop anywhere else.

Littleborough	15:13
Birchfield	–
Ashtown Parkway	–
Ashtown Central	16:00

I want to get from Littleborough to Ashtown Central as quickly as possible!

Aki

How much quicker is it for Aki to catch the express train than one of the other trains?

I am going to work out how long each journey is before finding the difference.

I think there is a quicker way. I can compare the departure and arrival times of the two journeys.

207

→ Practice book 5B p151

End of unit check

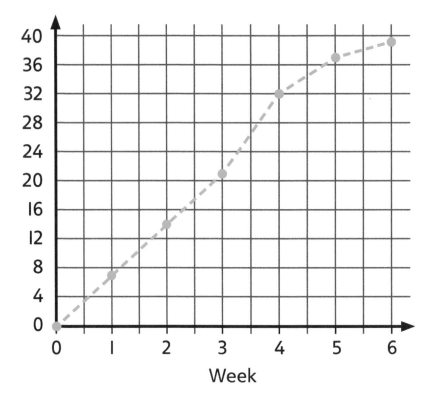

Height of sunflower in cm

Week

1 What is the height of the sunflower after 2 weeks?

A 12 cm   B 13 cm   C 14 cm   D 15 cm

2 How many cm does the flower grow between the start of Week 3 and the start of Week 5?

A 16 cm   B 21 cm   C 39 cm   D 60 cm

3 100 children were asked to choose their favourite sport.

How many children chose other sports?

A 0   C 41

B 31   D I cannot work it out.

Sport	Number of children
Football	40
Hockey	17
Rounders	12
Other sports	

4 How many more children chose football than rounders?

A 23   B 28   C 38   D 52

5 Here is part of a bus timetable.

How long does it take to get from Seagrove to Oaktown?

Seagrove	15:55
Woodfield	16:12
Oaktown	16:33

A 33 minutes   B 17 minutes   C 38 minutes   D 21 minutes

6 The table shows the number of people in a show.

	Singers	Dancers
Children	12	23
Adults	15	14

A member of the audience says, 'Over a quarter of the people in the show are adult singers.'

Is this true or false? Explain your answer.

→ Practice book 5B p154

There were lots of new things to learn. Sometimes I made mistakes but I will keep trying until I get it right!

Remember there is often more than one way to solve a problem. Look for other methods.

I enjoy listening to my partners to learn from them.

It is great to share ideas!

What have we learnt?

Can you do all these things?

⚡ Multiply a 4-digit number by a 2-digit number

⚡ Multiply fractions

⚡ Understand decimals and percentages

⚡ Calculate perimeter and area

⚡ Draw and interpret line graphs and tables

Some of it was difficult, but we did not give up!

Now you are ready for the next books!

POWER MATHS

White Rose Maths

Year 5 Textbook 5C

POWER MATHS

White Rose Maths

Year 5 Practice Book 5C

Published by Pearson Education Limited, 80 Strand, London, WC2R 0RL.

www.pearsonschools.co.uk

Text © Pearson Education Limited 2018, 2022
Edited by Pearson and Florence Production Ltd
First edition edited by Pearson, Little Grey Cells Publishing Services and Haremi Ltd
Designed and typeset by Pearson, Florence Production Ltd and PDQ Digital Media Solutions Ltd
First edition designed and typeset by Kamae Design
Original illustrations © Pearson Education Limited 2018, 2022
Illustrated by Laura Arias, Fran and David Brylewski, Diego Diaz, Virginia Fontanabona, Nadene Naude at
Beehive Illustration, Kamae Design, Florence Production Ltd, and PDQ Digital Media Solutions Ltd
Cover design by Pearson Education Ltd
Front and back cover illustrations by Diego Diaz and Nadene Naude at Beehive Illustration

Series Editor: Tony Staneff
Lead author: Josh Lury
Authors (first edition): Liu Jian, Josh Lury, Zhu Dejiang, Neil Jarrett, Timothy Weal, Zhu Yuhong, Caroline Hamilton,
Faye Hirst, Stephanie Kirk and Emily Fox
Consultants (first edition): Professor Liu Jian and Professor Zhang Dan

The rights of Tony Staneff and Josh Lury to be identified as authors of this work have been asserted by them in
accordance with the Copyright, Designs and Patents Act 1988.

First published 2018
This edition first published 2022

26 25 24 23
10 9 8 7 6 5 4 3

British Library Cataloguing in Publication Data
A catalogue record for this book is available from the British Library

ISBN 978 1 292 41958 9

Printed in the UK by Ashford Colour Press Ltd

For Power Maths resources go to
www.activelearnprimary.co.uk

Note from the publisher
Pearson has robust editorial processes, including answer and fact checks, to ensure the accuracy of the content in this
publication, and every effort is made to ensure this publication is free of errors. We are, however, only human, and
occasionally errors do occur. Pearson is not liable for any misunderstandings that arise as a result of errors in this
publication, but it is our priority to ensure that the content is accurate. If you spot an error, please do contact us at
resourcescorrections@pearson.com so we can make sure it is corrected.